ONE JERUSALEM: 1967–1977

ONE
JERUSALEM
1967–1977

Yael Guiladi

 KETER BOOKS

ACKNOWLEDGMENTS and thanks are due to the following institutions and persons for having kindly permitted the publisher to reproduce their photographs and illustrations: N. Avigad; Meir Ben-Dov; W. Braun; David Eisenberg; A.B. Glick; Government Press Office; Institute of Archaeology, Hebrew University; Israel Department of Antiquities; Israel Exploration Society; Israel Museum; The Jerusalem Foundation; Jewish National Fund; Keren Hayesod, United Israel Appeal; David Kroyanker; Photo Albert; David Radovan; Dan Shefner; Jac Susana; and others.

Cat. no. 25725 7
ISBN 0 7065 1580 3

Set, printed and bound by Keterpress Enterprises, Jerusalem
Printed in Israel

CONTENTS

A
CITY
REBORN

To THE detached chronicler, ten years in the multi-millennia saga of Jerusalem might well appear as just a little more than nothing and, taking a cold look at history, he could consider it presumptuous to concentrate on a single decade in the city's long, turbulent life. In the contemporary view, however, the prodigious changes which have taken place in Jerusalem between 1967 and 1977 confer upon this period a significance which greatly surpasses the sole limitations of time.

Those who recall the sight of Jerusalem during the 19 tragic years when a solid wall of hostility and fear divided it against itself, today find themselves expressing, each in his own manner, the spirit of the prophetic verse engraved by an anonymous Jew into the monumental stones of the Temple Mount over 1,000 years ago: "And when ye see this, your heart shall rejoice, and your bones shall flourish like young grass" (*Isaiah,* 66:14). For what they see is a city reborn. In place of the blind ugly concrete wall that cut through the heart of it, a myriad roses bloom. Yellow signs no longer block every east–west road, their skull and crossbones and thick black letters—"Halt! Danger! Frontier Ahead!"—terrifying children in search of a runaway ball. Their desolate emplacements have vanished among elegant residential suburbs, freshly planted gardens and newly paved

1

THE WESTERN APPROACHES TO THE OLD CITY

1948–1967: Blocked by a wall and the ruins of no-man's land huddling at the foot of the Old City ramparts.

1967: Opened up after the wall and the hovels had been removed.

1968–1975: Under reconstruction.

1977: "And when ye see this, your heart shall rejoice, and your bones shall flourish like young grass."

roads on which busy traffic moves in both directions across the old
divide. And the soldiers of the Arab Legion who, from atop Suleiman
the Magnificent's mighty walls, trained their gunsights on the city's
main roads, making every passing citizen a target, have disappeared
forever. Today, the Jews and Arabs of Jerusalem mingle freely, pur-
suing their activities, together or side by side, in a pragmatic spirit
of co-existence.

Since June 7, 1967 the Western Wall of the Temple Mount, Jewry's
holiest site, has not been deserted for a single moment, by day or by
night—a striking contrast to Ottoman or Mandatory days when
the Jew approached it furtively in fear of his life or, worse, when
under Jordanian rule access to it was completely denied him, and
public latrines were built beside its hallowed stones. The piles of
refuse which for years had been allowed to accumulate nearby have
at last been removed, and from beneath them archaeologists have
unearthed remains of no less than eight civilisations whose value
to world culture is inestimable. As for the Jewish Quarter, reduced
to a pile of rubble by the Jordanians, it has been almost entirely reconstructed in just ten years. Once again it blends intimately with
its surroundings, and its synagogues hum with the devotions of the
faithful after the 19-year break in their age-long tradition.

The dynamic activity triggered in all walks of life and among all
sections of the population by the reunification of Jerusalem has
wrought a profound change in the city's character. From an enclave
which for many led only to Heaven; a town whose western half
was blocked from north, south and east, cutting it off from its natural
hinterland; a site that was militarily insecure; a city whose life
was lived as a small, peripheral appendage of a country which, in
Israel's case, helped support its existence artificially, and in Jordan's,
left it to stagnate as a provincial backwater; a place that went to
bed early and from which one "escaped" to Tel Aviv or to Amman—
Jerusalem has acquired the air of a thriving metropolis with all its

attendant characteristics. From all over the world tourists flock to it, some for the pleasure of contemplating its beauty now that its scars have been healed, its monuments restored, its gardens replanted and its past revealed, others for religious reasons now that complete freedom of worship is guaranteed them. In fact, most of them come for a combination of both, for in Jerusalem the secular and the religious intertwine.

As a city holy to the three monotheistic faiths, Jerusalem has always enjoyed a privileged status in the hearts and minds of many men. Whatever their degree of orthodoxy, the mere name "Jerusalem" evokes some sort of memory or response. For the Moslem, it might be the image of the tale told to him in childhood of Mohammed flying from Jerusalem to Heaven on his legendary winged steed—"larger than a donkey, smaller than a mule" as one of the many traditions has it; or his adult desire to make the journey to the El Aksa mosque, Islam's third holiest shrine, if he could not fulfill the Prophet's injunction to accomplish the sacred Hadj to Mecca.

To the Christian, Jerusalem as a geographical entity naturally calls to mind the holy sites associated with the life and death of Christ and, as he follows in the footsteps of the Master, he finds himself in close communion with his spiritual origins. However, the significance of the city in Christian thought is more powerful through its identification with the Millennium, as St. John described it in his Revelation. In this sense, it is not necessarily confined to the physical limits of the terrestrial city. Spiritual Jerusalem can exist everywhere or, as St. Jerome put it: "The heavenly sanctuary is open from Britain no less than from Jerusalem, for the Kingdom of God is within you."

Jewish thought expresses quite the contrary conception. In the Talmud we can read this: "You also find that there is a Jerusalem above, corresponding to the Jerusalem below. For sheer love of the earthly Jerusalem, God made himself one above." Or again, these words placed in the mouth of God himself: "I will not enter heavenly

Jerusalem until I have entered the earthly Jerusalem first." Thus, we find the twin ideas of celestial and terrestrial Jerusalem closely linked. Indeed, since the time when David made Jerusalem his capital, turning it into a religious and national centre, this dual significance has been anchored in Jewish consciousness. The Prophets, whether they rejoiced or lamented, worked the city of Jerusalem, the land and the Jewish people into one great symbolic whole so that, in the course of time, Jerusalem as a geographical term also came to be used for naming an historical entity. History and religion thus remained linked to a concrete centre from which their origins sprung, towards which their prayers were turned during the exile and dispersion, and to which the ultimate return was deemed inevitable.

There is hardly a prayer in Jewish liturgy which at some point does not refer to the rebuilding of Jerusalem, and even the Jew who prays only once a year on the Day of Atonement repeats the 2,000-year-old yearning to be "Next year in Jerusalem." Every Jewish family is founded to the sound of the wedding benediction which likens Jerusalem, or Zion as it is frequently called, to the all-embracing mother: "Blessed art Thou, O Lord, who makest Zion joyful through her children." Liturgical devotion, popular piety, religious symbolism and messianic hope, even in their modern secular form, are directed first and foremost to the earthly Jerusalem as a symbol of the ingathering on this earth of the people to their promised land. Jerusalem thus has a value in itself. It is a geographical term beyond geography, but not without geography. It is the local habitation and the name for an historic existence and its continuity, an existence which for the religious Jew has religious dimensions, and which for the secular Jew is capable of a secularised expression.

The holiness of Jerusalem to the three religions was succinctly summed up by Professor Krister Stendahl when he wrote in the Harvard Divinity Bulletin in the autumn of 1966, "For Christians and Muslims that term (scil. holy sites) is an adequate expression of what

Celestial Jerusalem as it was depicted in a 14th-century German minia-
ture. Four figures with birds heads, wearing Jewish hats and prayer
shawls, are pointing upwards to the heavenly city, whose name appears in Hebrew characters to the right of the central tower.

matters. Here are sacred places, hallowed by the most holy events, here are the places for pilgrimage, the very focus of highest devotion . . . But Judaism is different . . . The sites sacred to Judaism have no shrines. Its religion is not tied to 'sites' but to the land, not to what happened in Jerusalem but to Jerusalem itself."

The spectacular revival of Jerusalem in the last ten years stems undoubtedly from the significance the city has held throughout the ages for all Jews, everywhere. Since the days of the Second Temple, when Herod lavished his legendary talents as a builder upon the city, it has not enjoyed such a period of expansion. Under each of its successive conquerors it was refashioned according to the circumstances of the times, but never did it represent more than a provincial centre. The moment their orderly return to it became feasible, the Jews streamed back to Jerusalem. From the second half of the 19th century their numbers grew steadily, more than doubling in the first half of the 20th to reach 100,000 in 1947. During that period, their proportion of the city's total population was roughly a constant two-thirds, the remainder being composed of Christians and Moslems. In 1949, Jerusalem became once again the capital of a sovereign Jewish state, and by 1967 its population had increased to 200,000 Jews and the constant third—70,000—Christians and Moslems. Today, ten years after reunification, the city has a population of 365,000 souls, 269,000 of them Jews, constituting three-quarters of the total, and 96,000 non-Jews. It is now the largest city in Israel and, since its decade of overall administration by a Jewish majority, it has acquired the status and dimensions worthy of its place in world civilisation in general, and Jewish life in particular.

Today, those seeking God can find Him without let or hindrance, and can worship in a spirit of freedom and tolerance unknown in the city for centuries. Those who seek a link with the past can find vestiges of each of the great civilisations which marched across Jerusalem, from early Hebrew and later Jewish of Second Temple times through Roman, Byzantine, Omayyad, Crusader and Mameluke down to Ottoman Turk. As for those who seek pure natural beauty on the rolling upland ridge between the gentle Mediterranean coast and the stark inland desert, or in the glowing gold of Jerusalem's stones, the force of its brilliant sunlight, the fragrance of its bracing night air and the clarity of its mountain moon, they are rarely disappointed.

The more down-to-earth find other fields of interest in the city. Many seek to study the social and cultural diversity of its inhabitants: erstwhile German professors, Moroccan artisans or Russian musicians; Arab intellectuals and Old City vendors; or the turbaned qadis, mitred monks and bearded rabbis, all of whom make up the tapestry of the Jerusalem scene. Whoever wishes to meet Israel's President, visit its parliament, deal with its government ministries and other national institutions, or attend its oldest university must come to the capital. Travellers find its geographical situation ideal as a junction between the cities of the West Bank, between Israel and the West Bank and thence across the open bridges over the Jordan into the Arab world. Architects, planners and builders are fascinated by the activity being deployed all over Jerusalem and by the challenge which rebuilding such a city involves: how to preserve everything connected with the past, maintain the natural and historical features of the city, and respect the interests of every religious trend within it, while at the same time transforming it into a modern capital which will be as free as possible of the plagues of 20th century urbanisation, and will remain a pleasant place for its inhabitants to live in.

Mediaeval maps placed Jerusalem at the centre of the world. Today such a conception is absurd, but one might envisage the city as the focus of concentric circles of interest. The first is formed around the Holy Places by the ever-present guardians of the respective faiths. The next encompasses inhabitants of the city, Jews and Arabs, whose active interest in all matters affecting it constitutes an outstanding

Turbaned qadis, bearded rabbis, simple citizens . . .

feature of the capital's life today. The third ring comprises Israel's
citizens who, for religious or secular reasons, make the "ascent" to
Jerusalem at various times of the year, their inordinate pride in their
capital's development often tinged with regret that they are not fortunate enough to live there. The next circle lies beyond Israel's borders
and encompasses the family of world Jewry which, by its constant

visits to, and material support for Jerusalem, expresses its link with it in the most concrete manner. Finally, there is the broad community of nations, those whose religious and cultural origins spring from the Judeo-Christian tradition or its Moslem outgrowth, and for all of whom Jerusalem bears a deeply rooted significance.

Those involved today in Jerusalem's development are well aware of the universal interest generated by everything connected with their accomplishments. They are also acutely conscious of the heavy responsibility they bear towards the past, the present and the future. It is not easy to administer an entity whose roots lie in the bedrock of history and whose branches lead to Heaven. The following pages will endeavour to describe the aims and achievements of those who for one decade have wholeheartedly devoted themselves to the re-unification and reconstruction of Jerusalem.

URBAN
TRANSFORMATION

A VISITOR TOURING Jerusalem for the first time in 1977 would have the utmost difficulty finding traces of the old frontier that severed it—should he be so perverse as to go looking for them! Immediately after the end of hostilities in June, 1967, and the removal by the Engineering Corps of the minefields across no-man's land, municipal authorities moved through the city, battered down the barriers, removed the barbed wire, and within a matter of days cleaned, paved and reconnected the main east–west roads across the area under their jurisdiction. By the festival of *Shavuot* (Pentecost) which fell on June 15, barely a week after the reunification of the city, the way was open to the unprecedented volume of human traffic which began flowing non-stop in both directions. Spontaneously the Jews went first to the Western Wall in a kind of collective, national act of faith, and from there, on to discover the Jewish Quarter and the Arab section of Jerusalem with which they had had no contact since 1948. The Arabs, following their example, undertook a voyage of rediscovery westward, first to Israel's capital and thence to the rest of Israel.

Once the immediate relinking of the city had been achieved, Government officials and city planners turned their attention to its large-scale reunification, reconstruction and development. Their

13

"And the wall . . .

. . . came tumbling down."

Mamilla Street, one of the main east—west roads through the heart of Jerusalem.

most obvious objectives were to erase all traces of the city's division, and to protect, preserve and restore all its historical and religious sites. The only changes envisaged within the Old City itself were the reconstruction of the Jewish Quarter and the clearing of an open space in front of the Western Wall to accommodate the throngs who flocked to it after 19 years of separation.

On the other hand, the immediate incorporation within the city's population of some 70,000 Arab citizens as well as the estimated inflow of new inhabitants, Jewish immigrants and Israelis, attracted by the beauty and character of their reunited capital, posed the problem of developing a modern, viable city within and around its ancient core. There could be no question of divorcing the contemporary from the historical, no thought of setting aside one section of the city as a cold museum, while beside it erecting a soulless agglomeration. Nor could uncontrolled building be permitted to disfigure the gently rolling landscape of Jerusalem's hills, to block its vistas westward to the Mediterranean and eastward to the desert, or to break the harmony of its ochre rocks from which for centuries the city has appeared to grow. At all times, planners were guided by the idea of making Jerusalem a living organism in which past, present and future would be closely integrated, its man-made elements blending into its natural features and this, no matter how thorny the practical urbanistic problems involved.

In their deliberations the city fathers have been, and are still, greatly assisted by the international Jerusalem Committee set up at the initiative of Mayor Teddy Kollek in 1969 as a body which would reflect and give expression to the significance of Jerusalem beyond Israel's borders. The Committee is made up of some 70 outstanding friends of the city who spontaneously accepted the city's invitation to join this voluntary world council. The Committee is concerned with the beautification and restoration of the city, as well as with its cultural content. Its members include clergymen, architects, town

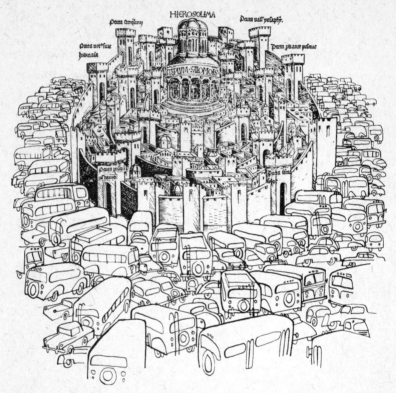

What planners have tried to avoid in developing a modern viable city around Jerusalem's ancient core.

planners, artists, politicians, university professors, theologians, sculptors, philosophers, publishers and archaeologists from all parts of the world. They meet at two- or three-yearly intervals to formulate their advice and criticism which they profer in a frank, objective manner. The experience of these outstanding personalities in all fields of human endeavour has helped Jerusalem's administrators to avoid some of the errors committed during the postwar period by town planners in other cities, and has placed at their disposal a wealth of talent on which they can freely draw.

The concept of an overall plan for the city which became feasible after its reunification inevitably involved the reallocation of certain stretches of land all over the city, and the redefinition of its uses. Shifting of inhabitants was kept to a minimum, but where there was no choice but to move them, compensation was paid on the basis of current market values, and alternative accommodation provided for those wishing to take advantage of it. In the case of land owned by institutions or churches, long delicate negotiations were entered into for the payment of compensation. As a rule, land owned by the Waqf, the executive arm of the Supreme Moslem Religious Council, has not been appropriated.

One of the highrisers which aroused severe public criticism. It obscures a magnificent view towards the Mount of Olives, and defigures the city's low-profile skyline.

One of the most important determinants of the city's future was the decision limiting its population. At a present level of 365,000, its eventual growth within the city limits is to be fixed at 650,000, composed as at present of 75 per cent Jews, and the remainder Christians and Arabs. The practical result of this will be that half the present municipal area of 25,000 acres will be built up, the other half being reserved for gardens and open spaces. Thus, Jerusalem will not reach unmanageable proportions and will retain a certain physical and social cohesion, qualities which are frequently lost once a city is allowed to grow unchecked.

After considerable discussion, triggered mainly by severe public criticism both from Jerusalem's own citizens and from its friends in Israel and abroad, two other basic decisions have been taken: first, no further throughways will be built in the city itself, a measure designed as much to protect citizens from pollution and noise as to limit traffic pressure on the city centre, particularly around the Old City; second, no further building beyond eight storeys in height will be permitted. This resolution was passed following the mushrooming of a number of highrisers fairly close to the Old City, plans for which had been approved before the city's reunification. Unanimously considered to be blots on the landscape, they obscure magnificent views and disfigure the low-profile skyline. As a result of this decision, a number of financially profitable projects have had either to be shelved, or completely redesigned.

At an early stage in the planning process, there was much talk of the demolition of Jerusalem's older quarters to make way for modern construction. Fortunately, those who recognised the historical and sociological value which the varied character of Jerusalem's neighbourhoods represents, succeeded in reversing this tendency. Today architects concentrate on preserving the external appearance of existing suburbs, contenting themselves with installing modern amenities behind their picturesque facades. A similar course of action is followed for isolated buildings, of which about 1,000 have been listed for preservation.

The stroller through Jerusalem cannot help noticing the considerable areas which have been set aside for parks and open spaces. This is no accident, but the result of a deliberate policy implemented by the city for both aesthetic and economic reasons. Thus, the National Park being created around the Old City walls is intended to enhance the beauty of the site, at the same time protecting its immediate environs from the ravages of unbridled economic exploitation. Similar considerations were behind the recent purchase by the Municipality from the Greek Orthodox Church, at great expense, of the Nikephoria area south of the King David Hotel. When laying out new suburbs, town planners try wherever possible to build on the ridges of the city's hilly contours, preserving the valleys for open spaces.

As in any living city, Jerusalem's neighbourhoods differ greatly, as much as a result of its past development as of its heterogeneous population. It is with greenery, rather than with cement, that its urbanists aim to join these varied elements together, starting from the city's heart and progressing from it.

REUNIFICATION

THE NATIONAL PARK

The exceptional character of the Old City, the wealth of architectural gems it houses, its historical and spiritual significance to millions, and the sheer physical beauty of its emplacement, clearly require special attention by all those engaged in the reunification of Jerusalem. In order to protect the *intra muros* area, one of the few remaining examples in the world of a completely walled town, the Municipality decided in 1967 to surround it with a National Park. Thus, not only would its superb Ottoman walls, constructed in the

THE OLD CITY'S OTTOMAN WALLS

1967: Desolation.

1977: Enhanced by the National Park.

16th century by Suleiman the Magnificent, be set off to greatest advantage, but also the area around them would be protected from the construction of buildings which would dwarf them, highways which would damage them, and other elements which could have an adverse effect on their character and scale. Free access to the city would be assured and the view towards it would remain unobstructed from all directions.

Of a total area of 750 acres, the Park is an ambitious project which will take many years to complete. Besides the immediate area around the walls, it includes the Valley of Hinnom, Mount Zion, the Ophel, the old City of David, the Pool of Siloam, the Valley of Kidron, Gethsemane, the slopes of the Mount of Olives and those of Mount Scopus, thus drawing the city's heart into one organic whole. In addition, the large-scale excavations at the southern and western walls of the Temple Mount, of which more will be said later in these pages, are to be included within it in the form of an archaeological garden.

So far the Ottoman walls have been repaired, the graftings onto them removed, their 34 towers and seven gates cleaned, and the promenade around the ramparts made safe. The stones used in this work were taken from the quarries used by Suleiman himself. In some areas, topsoil has been removed to expose the walls' lower courses. One kilometre of the pedestrian promenade which will eventually lead right round the Old City has already been laid, and magnificent floodlighting illuminates the walls into an almost theatrical spectacle by night. In order not to upset the delicate balance achieved by the use of different shades of lighting to accentuate the Citadel, towers and various neighbouring monuments, neon and mercury signs are prohibited in the area.

In the bed of the Hinnom and Kidron valleys which border the Old City on three sides, the Park is being planted with fig trees, vineyards, date palms and, of course, ancestral olive trees. Along the

The north-western approaches to the Old City which have yet to be restored in a manner befitting the character of the surroundings.

upper slopes, sparsely spaced in order to set off the contrasts of light and shade peculiar to the area, are to be pines and cypresses making dark green the dominant colour among the ochre rocks. Splashes of bougainvillea here and there will liven the composition. Only low shrubs, wild flowers and grass are allowed to grow at the foot of the walls so as not to conceal them. Along the western wall, between the Citadel and the south-west corner, recently discovered remains of the city's earlier fortifications will be incorporated into the garden, illustrating the major periods in the history of Jerusalem's walls.

The area adjacent to the Old City at its north-west corner, formerly at the heart of the 19-year-old divide and thus the most severely damaged, has not yet been completely restored in a manner befitting the character of the surroundings. The Notre Dame Hospice, partially destroyed during the 1948 war, has now been almost completely reconstructed by the Vatican. An innovation in its traditional role as a pilgrims' centre is to be a shopping arcade set into the facade opposite the Old City walls. There, religious articles and objets d'art will be sold, while the rest of the site will be developed as an arts and crafts centre. However, the remainder of the north-west area, known as Mamilla, as well as the terrain opposite Damascus Gate, has yet to be rebuilt. The urbanistic, economic and aesthetic problems involved are all part of the tangle the city fathers will have to unravel in order to complement the National Park complex, and complete the reunification of Jerusalem's heartland.

THE NORTHERN SUBURBS

Like the National Park, the large-scale development of the north and north-eastern suburbs since 1967 was conceived as a means of joining the severed city and erasing forever traces of its war-torn past. Symbolic was the return of the Hebrew University and the Hadassah Hospital to their original compounds on Mount Scopus. Though protected as a United Nations enclave, the buildings had been out of reach of their owners for 19 years and all activity within them paralysed. Today, the city continues uninterrupted from what was its former north-eastern border through the suburbs of Ramot Eshkol, Givat Hamivtar and Givat Shapira to the site of the old university campus, now rebuilt and greatly extended. It is indeed difficult to recall that until 1967 this entire area was honeycombed with bunkers and fortifications, only one example of which has been preserved for posterity at Givat Hatahmoshet (Ammunition Hill).

The style of the north and north-eastern suburbs is not uniform, and building heights vary from one to four storeys in accordance with the lie of the land. One of the notable features of the new neigh-

bourhoods is the traditional Jerusalem inner courtyard around
which the modern apartment blocks are set. Promenades, playgrounds
and car parks fill the open spaces thus formed. The extensive use of
this architectural form was made in an attempt to break with the
norms of suburban construction and integrate the area within its
surroundings. Similarly, facades are frequently decorated with arched
windows, vaulted porticos and colourful mosaics. In Ma'alot Daphna,
south of Ammunition Hill even more daring combinations have
been tried: motorised traffic has been separated from pedestrian
walks which lead through shopping arcades into squares and piazzas;
design is largely assymetrical and incorporates protruding elements
and sloping roofs finished with stone. The meeting point for the north-
eastern suburbs' 24,000 inhabitants lies in a hollow between the eastern
and western ridges. It is composed of highrise buildings, and houses

The shopping centre of the north-eastern suburbs.

an extensive shopping area, public buildings, parks and playgrounds.

The reconstruction of the Mount Scopus campus on land owned by the Hebrew University for over 50 years represented a challenge in itself. It was to be large, yet compact; it had to be moulded around the topography of the land in such a way as to preserve the ridge's skyline, and it had to achieve a gradual transition from the open National Park area on the lower slopes to the densely built-up complex on the hilltop. But above all, the breathtaking panorama which stretches from the crest of Scopus eastward over the Judaean Desert to the Dead Sea, and westward to the Old City and the rest of Jerusalem, had to be preserved.

The plan is now in an advanced stage of execution and would seem to have fulfilled most of the criteria. Eventually, the Mount Scopus campus will cater to some 18,000 students, with accommodation facilities for 5,000 unmarrieds and 800 families. It will house the Faculties of Humanities and Social Studies, the exact sciences remaining

The Mount Scopus campus is moulded around the ridge in such a way as to preserve its skyline.

at Givat Ram in western Jerusalem, the alternative campus that was
built during the years when Mount Scopus was inaccessible. Because
of the limitations imposed by the National Park on the western
slopes of the ridge, future development will be towards the east.

INDUSTRIAL ZONES

Though more will be said later in these pages about Jerusalem's
industrial development and economic integration since 1967, it is
worthy of note in this context that two of the three industrial zones
established in the last ten years are located in the former border
areas of Talpioth and Sanhedria. Once partially deserted, these zones
now abound with economic activity and act as a solid unifying element. The third centre, Atarot, is situated on the city's present
northern border and, like the other two, is making a valid contribution to the capital's economic integration.

OTHER ASPECTS OF REUNIFICATION

Not all the elements involved in the reunification of Jerusalem
have been as striking as the Mount Scopus campus or the National
Park. After the cessation of hostilities in 1967, water and sewerage
networks were immediately reconnected at points where they had
been joined during Mandatory times. This done, however, the Municipality found itself confronted with the enormous task of raising the
level of services in the eastern sector to that customary in all cities in
Israel. Neither the British nor the Jordanian authorities who had administered east Jerusalem since 1929 had made any serious effort to
modernise the infrastructure of the Old City, with the result that in
1967 some of its inhabitants were still living in mediaeval conditions,
drawing water from wells or communal taps. All this was very picturesque, but hardly in keeping with 20th-century concepts of health,

hygiene and living standards. Today, ten years later, 90 per cent of east Jerusalem homes, both within and without the *intra muros* area, have running water installations connected to the main city supply. The expense incurred proved too onerous for the residents themselves and was met almost entirely by the Municipality.

Within the Old City itself, a direct consequence of this radical change in living conditions was to render the existing sewerage-cum-drainage system, a relic of Turkish times, hopelessly inadequate to cope at the same time with the increased flow of waste and torrential winter rains, a situation liable to create flooding. The separation of the two networks poses a thorny problem which is further complicated by the fact that the character of the Old City makes any kind of underground work extremely difficult to accomplish. Modern machines are often too large to penetrate its narrow alleyways, and not precise enough to prevent possible damage to its ancient structures. Much of the work has therefore to be done by hand, and at very great expense. A major attempt at renewing the sewerage system in the Old City is now under way in the Moslem Quarter. As part of this project, all electrical, telephone and television cables will be installed underground. The situation is less critical outside the Old City. In the northern and eastern suburbs of east Jerusalem, entirely new sewerage networks have been laid, and where installations already existed, they have been repaired. This has put the inhabitants of such areas as Atarot, the At-Tur village on the Mount of Olives and the former refugee camp at Anatot within reach of an adequate waste disposal system if they desire to connect up with it.

Electricity has always been, and continues to be, supplied to the eastern sector of Jerusalem by an Arab company whose concession, renewed by Israel authorities since reunification, covers a radius of 20 kilometres around the Church of the Holy Sepulchre. Beyond that limit, the Municipality deemed it essential to connect the entire area within its jurisdiction to the main city electricity supply, this at its own expense. At the time of writing,some 85 per cent of this work has been completed, providing every householder with the possibility of connecting his home to the main supply line.

A similar course has been adopted with regard to the road network. Apart from the relinking of arterial roads across the city's central area, all 14 villages which fall within the municipal jurisdiction have been connected to the nearest main artery. This, added to the running water, street lighting, electricity and the developing drainage system, represents a vast improvement in the daily life of many hundreds of the city's Arab citizens, and has gone far in bringing their living conditions closer to those enjoyed by their Jewish fellow citizens.

RECONSTRUCTION

THE JEWISH QUARTER

The restoration of the Jewish Quarter of the Old City is perhaps the best example of how the general principles underlying the reconstruction of Jerusalem as a whole have been applied. Neither wholly museum, which it might have become considering the spectacular finds revealed by archaeologists before building began, nor wholly religious, as its close proximity to Judaism's most holy site could have made it, the Jewish Quarter today is a picturesque ensemble in which each significant element has its place. Its inhabitants—artists and rabbis, Yeshiva students and businessmen, simple citizens and descendants of its former residents—mingle with the tourists among its winding alleys, its restored synagogues and Crusader ruins exactly as their forefathers did. That the Jews chose to settle in the south-eastern corner of the walled enclave on their return to the city after the Crusader period was only natural, since of the four quarters into which the Old City was divided by the Roman north–south and east–west axes, it was the closest to the remains of the Second Temple.

Each of the other three quarters has since been inhabited by the Christian, Moslem and Armenian communities, respectively.

The Jewish Quarter as it is known today covers some 25 acres. Bordered in the north by the Street of the Chain, in the west by the Armenian Quarter, and in the south by the Ottoman city wall, its eastern slopes face the Temple Mount and adjacent to it, the hallowed Western Wall. Records of its synagogues go back as far as the 13th century, and testimony left by travellers through the centuries show that the fortunes of its population varied at the whim of its rulers, at times thriving, at others reduced to the depths of misery.

In the mid-19th century, some 7,000 Jews were living in the Old City, just under half its total population, but 50 years later their number had more than doubled, making them a majority within the

The Old City—an architectural pattern into which the reconstructed Jewish Quarter had to be woven.

intra muros area. It was at this period, however, that Jewish settlement outside the city walls was conceived as a means of alleviating living conditions in the crowded, insanitary Jewish Quarter. As a result both of this, and of the anti-Jewish outbreaks of 1936–7, its population dwindled rapidly, and by the end of the British Mandate in 1948, only 2,000 Jews were still living there.

When the Israelis returned to the Quarter in 1967, a scene of desolation confronted them. The ruins of some 60 synagogues were found desecrated, former public buildings had been wantonly destroyed, and in the few houses still standing among the debris squatters had found slum lodgings. The restoration and repopulation of the Jewish Quarter was decided upon shortly afterwards. All those found living there were paid compensation, the exact sum having been fixed by negotiation and according to such objective considerations as the size of the family and its living conditions. In addition, easy credit facilities, similar to those offered Jewish home buyers, were made available to them for the purchase of new apartments, either in the modern housing estate constructed for them by Government and municipal bodies, or in the apartment blocks built by Arab contractors to rehouse them in east Jerusalem suburbs. In most cases, however, the families preferred to use their compensation to build themselves pleasant, modern houses of their own, in keeping with Arab custom. It is perhaps of interest to note that the Jordanian Government had drawn up a detailed plan to evict the squatters from the Jewish Quarter slums as far back as 1962, a process which was speeded up in 1966. It was thus only those who had ignored repeated Jordanian eviction orders who were still there in 1967. As for former Jewish residents of the Old City, those who could prove their right of ownership to property there were given the choice between acquiring a home in the reconstructed area on a preferential basis, or accepting compensation.

The team of architects who planned the reconstruction of the

Jewish Quarter had a long list of criteria to meet, the most important of which was to weave the area into the pattern of the Old City. While they aimed at creating an ordinary residential neighbourhood as the Quarter had always been, they could not ignore its traditional value and its proximity to the Western Wall, factors which naturally focus religious and tourist interest on it. The topography of the land on which the Quarter lies, its terraced slopes overlooking the splendid view of the Temple Mount and behind it, the Mount of Olives, had also to be taken into account. It was naturally also considered desirable to restore as much as humanly possible of existing remains, great as the expense involved would inevitably be. But before any work at all could be undertaken in the Quarter, the archaeologists had to be given the opportunity of revealing what was buried beneath it. Of their spectacular discoveries more will be said later in these pages. Insofar as the architects were concerned, their job was to integrate the finds within their plan of reconstruction, constantly modifying it as the excavations progressed.

To all these architectural considerations were added the down-to-earth problems of laying a completely new underground system of water piping, sewerage, electricity, telephone and television cables, and this under the particularly difficult working conditions in the Quarter. Transport could be effected only on donkey back, and much of the construction work had to be done by hand since access by large machinery is impossible in the area.

The end result is a unique composition made up of a network of narrow alleys closely woven into the texture of the buildings. It is the contrasting play of light and shade among the gaps in the masonry, the dark winding lanes leading into unexpected courtyards, and the arches, domes and vaults worked into its architecture that have helped create the Quarter's picturesque character. Its main shopping and tourist roadway, the Street of the Jews, lies along the north–south axis of the Old City, growing naturally out of the

The Old City's central market core out of which grows . . .

enclave's central market core. While construction of the area was in progress, remains of the Cardo, the original Roman north–south road, were revealed (see page 74). As a result, plans for the shopping gallery were modified to incorporate the finds beneath the commercial area. The Street of the Jews has been designed to maintain the existing rhythm of the northern bazaar by continuing its pattern of arches

... the Street of the Jews. It has been designed to maintain the existing architectural rhythm of arches and vaulted roofs through which the daylight filters.

and the effect of natural light filtering from above through the small apertures in the vaulted roof.

From this main route, two paths branch out and follow the mountain slope eastwards, finally meeting at the "Bazaar," a complex of underground vaults which have been restored to form another small commercial centre. Above them is a café commanding an impressive view over the Temple Mount and the Judaean hills beyond. A broad stairway leads from this square down the hillside to the Western Wall. As yet untouched, the eastern facade of the Quarter, lying as it does on a promontory overlooking the Temple Mount, will be incorporated within the overall plan for the Western Wall—of which more later.

Like the rest of the Old City, the Jewish Quarter is closed to vehicular traffic, essential services being provided by electrically powered, highly manoeuvrable vehicles. The 630 families for whom it has been planned will occupy about half its total area, the bulk of the remainder being devoted to public and religious institutions. These latter include some 60 synagogues and four main Houses of Study —Yeshivot—with an additional 1,500 residents. Of two to four storeys high, the residential quarters are built around inner courtyards shared by several families. The pyramidal style in which the buildings have been designed allows as much sunlight as possible to reach the ground, and their stepped form makes roofs available as passageways, courtyards and balconies. Wherever possible, the outer shells of existing buildings have been reinforced by subtle engineering devices in order to preserve their vaulted, cross-vaulted and domed roofs, and their arched window frames. In this way, the continuity of the Old City's character has been maintained.

Outstanding among the few buildings which were spared in the wholesale destruction of the Jewish Quarter by the Jordanians were the four Sephardic synagogues. At the time they were built, Jews were not permitted to erect structures that rose higher than those of the Moslems surrounding them. Ironically, it was this discriminatory measure which saved the buildings for, dug deep into the ground, they were partially concealed. Though their outer walls, roofs and domes were preserved, the synagogues were found completely gutted

THE JEWISH QUARTER, BEFORE AND AFTER

and, as a consequence of their use as goat pens for 19 years, the piles of refuse which had accumulated inside took almost one year to remove.

The exact origins of the Sephardic synagogues are obscure. However, there is evidence to suggest that the first of them was built in the 16th century on the site now known as the Yohanan ben Zakkai synagogue. From the original prayer hall, today considered to be the one called the Eliyahu Hanavi synagogue, the building grew into an interconnecting complex of four synagogues, each successive one having been added as the needs of the community grew. Their function, however, went well beyond that of mere houses of prayer. Throughout the centuries they were as much the focus of Sephardic religious observance as they were the centre of the community's charitable institutions, and of its spiritual and intellectual life.

In the 17th century, the synagogues were described by a Christian traveller as "the greatest and most beautiful in the Promised Land," but this golden age was shortlived. The arrival in the early 18th century of increasing numbers of old, poor Jews who had come to the city only to die placed a considerable burden on the community. Its situation deteriorated further at the end of the century; the synagogues fell into ruins, and their repair was prohibited by the local rulers. It was not until 1835 that the community obtained permission from the governor to renovate them, in spite of an old Moslem law prohibiting the construction and improvement of non-Moslem religious buildings.

The rapid development of the Jewish community in the Old City at the end of the 19th century greatly enhanced the importance of the Sephardic synagogues, restoring to them their role as the social and spiritual centre of all the Jews in the city. It was there that the Emperor Franz Joseph was welcomed to Jerusalem by the leaders of the Jewish community in 1870, and a protest meeting was held within their walls during the Beilis blood libel trial. In 1893, the

1967

1977

THE SEPHARDIC
SYNAGOGUES

An ancient tradition renewed.

inauguration ceremony of the Yishuv's chief rabbi took place for the first time in the Yohanan ben Zakkai synagogue, so that the entire community, Ashkenazi and Sephardi, could participate in it. The ancient prayer houses were used for the last time in 1948 as an underground shelter for those of the Jewish Quarter's inhabitants who had not fled the Arab attacks.

A stroller in the Jewish Quarter might well by-pass the four Sephardic synagogues. From the outside an unimpressive cluster of buildings, their entrances are modestly concealed, their domed roofs do not protrude above those surrounding them, they have no exterior windows, and their floors lie some three metres below street level. On descending into them one is therefore the more surprised by the majesty of their spacious halls, their lofty domes and their graceful Gothic arches.

Of no uniform style, the synagogues bear the mark of each of the periods in which they were built, and the origins of those who built them. The Yohanan ben Zakkai and the Emtzai synagogues are long, cross-vaulted structures, while in the Eliyahu Hanavi and the Istanbuli halls, four pillars support a windowed drum topped by a cupola. This structure is a derivative of Byzantine and early Islamic styles, though without their characteristic symmetry. There is clearly a Spanish influence in the shape of the windows of the Ben Zakkai and Istanbuli halls, their carved tops reflecting the Moorish "camel back" style. A further trace of the Moorish influence brought to Jerusalem by Jews of Spanish origin can be found in the Gothic front of the Holy Ark in the Ben Zakkai synagogue. The architects who restored the synagogues tried to preserve their Spanish style by replacing, in the two cupolas, stone-framed windows similar to those found in 12th-century Spanish synagogues. Following the ancient method, glass medallions of various shades were used, through which rays of sunlight filter across the interiors. Bronze doors designed by the winners of a contest now mark the modest entrances to the buildings, and furnishings to replace the sumptuous decorations destroyed in 1948 have been brought from Sephardic synagogues in Italy and Spain.

What is of greater significance, however, is the fact that today the four Sephardic synagogues have been restored to the heirs of their founders. In the course of their daily pursuits, the faithful can pass unmolested through their tranquil, sunlit halls and reflect on the glorious tradition which they have had the privilege to renew. Indeed, the same may be said of the entire Jewish Quarter whose links with history from the Iron Age on, now dramatically revealed, add a further dimension to its contemporary revival.

MISHKENOT SHA'ANANIM

The historical outgrowth of the Jewish Quarter is the neighbour-hood known as Mishkenot Sha'ananim and alongside, Yemin Moshe, so named after Moses Montefiore who was the first to conceive and carry out the settlement of Jews outside the Old City walls as from 1859. Built on the western slopes of the Hinnom Valley, the site commands a magnificent view of the Old City's western Ottoman walls, the Citadel at Jaffa Gate, and the divide in the Judaean hills leading down to the Dead Sea. During the 19 years of Jerusalem's division, Mishkenot Sha'ananim and Yemin Moshe constituted the first line of settlement beyond no-man's land, their inhabitants stubbornly remaining despite the sniping from the Old City walls to which they were frequently subjected throughout that period. Inevitably, because of the high security risk involved, little was done to improve the area, with the result that by 1967 it had become a poor, run-down neighbourhood.

With the reunification of the city, its value soared overnight. No sooner had hostilities ceased than potential purchasers were outbidding each other to obtain plots in the appropriated area.

Mishkenot Sha'ananim: from a rundown neighbourhood on the edge of no-man's land to a guest house for visiting artists. To the right lies Yemin Moshe, its refurbished homes set in a delightful ensemble of small squares, pocket parks, steps and olive trees.

Alternative housing or compensation was offered to its inhabitants, many of whom were grateful for the opportunity to purchase modern apartments elsewhere. Others left with less alacrity, regretting the loss of the spirit of social cohesion that had maintained the neighbourhood during its 19 dangerous years and, of course, "their" view.

Mishkenot Sha'ananim has now been converted into a residence for visiting artists. Its original ground plan—one-storeyed buildings made up of a series of one- or two-roomed dwellings, each with its own entrance—has been preserved. Thus each guest has a self-contained apartment, complete now with all modern facilities. An interesting feature of the structures is their crenellated facades, designed no doubt as an echo to the Ottoman walls across the valley. Around the buildings the landscape has been terraced so that the visitor, strolling in the rock gardens, can draw inspiration from the panorama—golden in daylight, purple at sunset—of the valley spread out before him.

Yemin Moshe too has been rebuilt principally as an artists' quarter, the facades of the original low-lying buildings having been meticulously preserved. Open only to pedestrians, the delightful ensemble of steps, small squares, pocket parks and olive trees mingles with the refurbished homes to form a tranquil neighbourhood through which Jerusalem's inhabitants can walk of an evening and admire the ethereal beauty of the illuminated Old City walls. Thanks to its faithful restoration, the Yemin Moshe quarter blends perfectly into the National Park which links it to the Old City in the east, and the Bloomfield Park in the Nekophoria area which lies between it and the modern city to the west.

THE JEWISH CEMETERY ON THE MOUNT OF OLIVES

The Jewish Cemetery on the Mount of Olives is the oldest and largest of Jewish graveyards: many were the faithful who throughout the ages made provision for their burial there, in order to be on the spot on the Day of Judgement. When the Jews returned to their hallowed burial place in 1967, they found that hundreds of consecrated graves had been uprooted to make way for a new road. Of the cemetery's 50,000 tombstones, 38,000 had been desecrated or stolen, many of them later found in surrounding villages where they had been laid as paving stones, or as floors for the latrines of Jordanian army camps. Adjacent to the National Park, the cemetery has now been restored, its tombstones replaced, and its grounds reconsecrated for their traditional use.

The hallowed Jewish cemetery on the Mount of Olives as it was found
in 1967. It had been wantonly desecrated by the Jordanians.

Jewish tombstones used in the construction of Jordanian Army barracks.

DEVELOPMENT

If, as expected, Jerusalem's population continues to increase at the present rate of 4 per cent annually, it will reach the half-million mark in 1987, doubling in the 20 years since reunification. It is therefore not surprising that new suburbs are mushrooming all over the municipal area. Apart from the north-eastern neighbourhoods already described, four major housing estates are being built along the city's northern and southern exurban periphery. On completion, Ramot and Neve Ya'akov in the north, Gilo and East Talpioth in the south, will house a total of 100,000 inhabitants, most of them immigrants, young couples or families moved from slum areas. Together with the housing schemes of Ramot Sharett and Givat Shaul under construction in the western suburbs, they are expected to accommodate 70 per cent of the Jewish population increase.

Since 1967, there has also been a considerable growth in private building by Jerusalem's Arab citizens. This expansion, some of it financed by some 5,000 mortgages granted by the Municipality, has been due in part to the natural population increase, in part to the influx of workers to the city during the building boom, and finally to the overall prosperity generated by the city's reunification. By tradition fundamentally different from the Jewish building patterns mentioned above, Arab construction is carried out on an individual basis, generally taking the form of small houses, or additions to existing ones. This type of building tends to be dispersed and is often put up without consultation of the master plan for the area concerned. In order to ensure that new housing should not become an obstacle in the way of east Jerusalem's future infrastructural development, it has now been decided to draw up a set of guidelines indicating where construction can be freely undertaken. In any event, urbanistic surveys show that sufficient land is available for undisturbed, low-density Arab housing development in the areas north and south of the Old City for a long time to come. Recently, the Municipality embarked upon its plan for the construction of several hundred housing units in east Jerusalem, this as part of its slum clearance programme.

The large-scale development of Jerusalem's residential areas clearly entails the expansion of its administrative and commercial core, projects to which much thought has been given.

THE GOVERNMENT PRECINCT

Situated on Kiryat Ben Gurion between the Knesset (Israel's Parliament) and the Convention Centre, Government Precinct has been the object of many development plans since 1948. The reunification of the city gave further impetus to the concentration of all national Government offices in this area within an architectural framework reflecting Jerusalem's significance as Israel's capital.

At the demographic centre of Jerusalem as it is today, the area is to be surrounded by a botanical garden, and all the valleys which fan out from it are to be incorporated within the city's inner green belt. While no final decision has yet been made concerning the form the Precinct will eventually take, the plan under discussion is composed of four highrise buildings to house the Prime Minister's Office and the Foreign, Finance and Interior Ministries, these to be surrounded by smaller constructions on the slope of the rise. The highrisers pose the fundamental question of the image to be given to the Precinct, a matter which is still the subject of a fierce debate. On its outcome will depend the aspect which the central Government complex of Israel's capital will finally present to its citizens.

A model of the proposed Civic Centre.

CIVIC CENTRE

The city's new Civic Centre is to be constructed in the Russian Compound at the very heart of central Jerusalem—meeting point between its eastern and western suburbs. It will comprise a new City Hall which, slightly higher than the surrounding buildings, will serve as a landmark, while the public and business offices will be housed in lower structures nestling around it. The complex will include a landscaped square and open spaces for pedestrian promenades.

THE CITY CENTRE

Jerusalem's city core presents a generally run-down appearance, hardly in keeping with the natural and architectural beauty of its surroundings. Detailed plans for its rehabilitation and expansion abound, but the formidable problems posed by the evacuation of existing tenants, and the payment of adequate compensation, make their application a complex, protracted and costly affair. Similar considerations are involved in the planning of an adequate road network and even in the possible transformation of Ben Yehuda

Street, one of the city's main commercial areas, into a pedestrian mall, this on account of the numerous taxi stands located on, or in close proximity to it. For the moment, then, the city is contenting itself with widening and linking existing roads and eventually reserving certain routes for public transport, the present ratio of 60 per cent public and 40 per cent private transport to be maintained in the future. The original plan for a north–south highway to pass through the heart of the city very close to the Old City walls has been definitively abandoned as a result of public protest, and will be replaced by a road that will pass west of the Givat Ram campus.

Current thinking on the central business area now runs along the lines of the preservation and restoration of existing constructions, rather than on their outright demolition. A delightful example of this is the Maskit building in the heart of the city. Formerly part of a

A picturesque Jerusalem facade selected for restoration.

printing press complex, the building has been completely restored, its stonework cleaned and repaired, and its wrought iron decorations replaced. The redesigned interior today houses a boutique for tourists while the courtyard, once part of the workshop, has been turned into a tree-shaded café which is greatly appreciated by tourists and Jerusalemites alike.

A similar policy is to be applied to whole neighbourhoods in the city centre, such as the old Nahlat Shiva quarter and the tree-shaded streets around the Coptic Church. By extension it will also comprise suburbs such as Bak'a with its magnificent, if run-down, villas, and the garden neighbourhood of the German Colony. Thus the varied characteristics of the city's historic quarters will be maintained, adding more to its charm than all the soulless modern office blocks designed for it.

The Mamilla area and that adjoining Damascus Gate have already been mentioned in connection with their proximity to the Old City and the National Park.

THE WESTERN WALL

Since its dramatic return to Jewish hands in 1967 the Western Wall, national and religious shrine of the Jewish people, has been the object of great concern to the civil, religious and national authorities. Though a final decision has yet to be reached as to exactly how its immediate surroundings are to be laid out, the project at present under discussion would seem to fulfill many of the criteria essential to the reconstruction of such a highly sensitive area.

As a first requisite, the project envisages the exposure of the Western Wall down to its original level when it was built as a retaining wall around the Second Temple Esplanade. The additional nine metres of imposing Herodian blocks thus revealed would greatly enhance the majesty of the site. In order not to dwarf it, the area

One of the proposals for the reconstruction of the area adjacent to the Western Wall.

between the Wall and the Jewish Quarter would be laid out in a series of ascending terraces, creating a gradual transition from the regal scale of the Wall to the smaller and more complex dimensions of the Jewish Quarter. The widest of the terraces would be that closest to the Wall, the others decreasing as they recede from it. Though this plan will encroach somewhat on the existing open space in front of the Wall, the terraces will in fact be able to accommodate a greater number of participants and spectators than the present area. It is perhaps of interest to note that in his *Antiquities,* written during the Second Temple period, the historian Josephus Flavius described the area west of the Temple Mount thus: "The city lay opposite the Temple in the form of a theatre." By this he probably meant that it was built in steps down the slope.

In order to prevent the pedestrian traffic which passes from the Dung Gate to other parts of the Old City from disturbing the sanctity of the site, a covered way with arched openings facing east towards the Wall would be incorporated behind the uppermost terrace. With similar discretion all the public facilities essential to such a highly frequented area—first aid, refreshments, restrooms, modest souvenir booths—have been provided for. Finally, an archaeological museum to house the wealth of objects found in the vicinity of the Wall is an integral part of the plan.

Whatever form this project finally takes, its primary objective will always be the preservation of the aura of sanctity which surrounds the Wall and which, beyond all architectural considerations, is and will remain its dominant characteristic.

THE
REMAINS
OF
HISTORY

SYMBOLIC LINK between all Jews in time and in space, the Western Wall acquired its sacred character because for centuries it was believed to be the only vestige of the Second Temple built by King Herod 2,000 years ago. The Temple's destruction at the hands of Titus on the ninth of Av in the year 70 C.E. marked the end of Jewish national life in Jerusalem for centuries to come, and the extent of the tragedy was such that its anniversary has been observed ever since in Jewish liturgy as a day of mourning. With access to the Temple Mount constantly denied to Jews by the city's various overlords, the Western Wall came in a sense to replace it. Today, the wealth and variety of unearthed remains of the Second Temple's outer building complex, of which the Western Wall is a part, have taken on staggering proportions; yet despite their splendour, the hallowed site has lost nothing of its sanctity.

Both historically and pragmatically, the area adjacent to the Western Wall was the obvious starting point for excavations in 1967. Totally neglected during the period of Jordanian rule, its surroundings were found defiled by latrines and piled high with the city's refuse. The south-west corner of the Temple Mount had in fact served for years as a municipal rubbish dump. As for the Jewish Quarter, its almost total destruction by the Jordanians gave the

53

archaeologists freedom to fully explore the area before reconstruction was allowed to begin.

That expectations were high was only natural: the earlier finds of European and American archaeologists who had worked on a limited scale in the areas west, south, and south-west of the Temple Mount were indications of what might still be there to discover. And then there were the tantalising descriptions of the Herodian edifice that were left to posterity by Josephus Flavius, chronicler of the times, to be confirmed or refuted once and for all. However, the uncovering of an entire building complex dating to the seventh century Omayyad period, whose existence was totally unknown, surpassed even the most optimistic previsions.

It may well seem to the layman, as he makes his way round the south-west corner of the Herodian walls, that he can simply bend

The south-western corner of the Temple Mount, 13 metres of giant Herodian blocks towering against the sky.

down and pick up three thousand years of history. Clearly exposed
before him are Jewish burial caves dating back to the First Temple
period, seven or eight centuries before Christ; a few steps eastwards,
and below the present ground level, lie the remains of the massive
building works with which Herod embellished the south-western and
southern approaches to the Temple Esplanade—monumental stair-
cases, wide, well paved streets lined with small shops, and a host of
remains attesting to the scale and beauty of the Royal Stoa which
ran all along the southern wall; slightly to the south appear the neat
traces of the encampment of the Tenth Roman Legion which occu-
pied the city after its destruction, and whose soldiers perhaps helped
build the famous Cardo, main north–south road of the Roman
city, recently uncovered in the Jewish Quarter. At a higher level
again, vestiges of spacious, early Christian dwellings of Byzantine
times are dotted over the area, while on the surface, at the foot of
the southern wall, stand the ruins of the splendid Omayyad palace
and its attendant buildings. A short walk just outside the Dung Gate
leads to Crusader fortifications, while westwards up in the Jewish
Quarter the remains of the Church of St. Mary of the Teutonic
Knights appear among the new constructions. By the time our
layman has reached the 16th-century Ottoman walls around the Old
City, he almost feels he is back in the modern era.

It would take many volumes to do justice to the excavations carried
out in Jerusalem since 1967 by a dedicated body of men under the
auspices of the Israel Exploration Society, the Hebrew University
and the Jerusalem Foundation. Their contribution to the history of
mankind is immense: in some cases they have revealed completely
new data, in others corrected erroneous ideas long held, or, con-
versely, confirmed existing theories. With scrupulous care they have
preserved intact vestiges of all periods and all civilisations, often at
great trouble and expense. Indeed, they have frequently foregone
the desire to push their shovels further down in order not to destroy

existing remains of later periods, or to infringe on hallowed shrines. Throughout the excavations around the Temple Mount, qualified engineers have exercised constant control in order to ensure that the site is in no way damaged by the archaeologists' work.

While a detailed survey of each and every find is beyond the scope of this work, no summary of life in Jerusalem would be complete without a description of the most outstanding among them, the more so since they have greatly marked the spirit of the city over the past decade.

FIRST TEMPLE PERIOD: 8TH–6TH CENTURY B.C.E.

Perhaps the most fascinating aspect of the earliest Iron Age finds unearthed on what the archaeologists call the Western Hill—today's Jewish Quarter—is the confirmation they provide of ancient Biblical texts. For many years a controversy raged among scholars as to the precise extent of Jerusalem during the First Temple period. Whilst the confines of the City of David were recognised as lying on the Eastern Hill—the rise south of the Temple Mount and west of the Kidron Valley—the exact site of the Mishne (second) Quarter mentioned in the Bible was never defined.

The most important discovery made in the recent excavations, therefore, is an impressive segment of an Israelite wall, 40 metres long and seven metres thick. Situated some 275 metres west of the Temple Mount, the wall runs from north-east to south-west, turning sharply west at its southern end, possibly to form a tower. At this point, it cuts right through the remains of a house dating from the same period. This would seem to confirm that settlement outside the City of David began as an unwalled quarter, presumably the Mishne, which only later was included within the fortifications of which the discovered wall constitutes a small section. The massive

Part of an Israelite city wall dating from the eighth century—the Iron Age—found in today's Jewish Quarter.

structure resembling a tower, and preserved to a height of eight metres, uncovered elsewhere in the Jewish Quarter, may well have been part of these same building works. The Bible mentions various kings who restored the walls of Jerusalem, but the description which best fits the evidence points to Hezekiah who around 700 B.C.E. "built up all the wall that was broken, and raised it up to the towers, and another wall without" (*Chronicles* 2, 32:5).

Though the long series of destructions and reconstructions of Jerusalem have left few actual remains of the First Temple period on the Western Hill, wall fragments, substructures and artifacts, all of the Iron Age period, clearly indicate Jewish settlement there in the seventh and eighth centuries before Christ—thus, for example, a store jar bearing a fine Hebrew inscription and thought to have been used to bring offerings to the nearby Temple; impressions of private seals clearly showing the names of their owners; and pottery remains, including figurines representing the fertility symbol.

A few months ago, for the first time after eight years of excavations near the southern wall of the Temple Mount, a most impressive First Temple structure was revealed, lying beneath an equally splendid Second Temple one! Destroyed no doubt by Nebuchadnezzar when he sacked Jerusalem in 568 B.C.E., the structure is over 70 metres long, some 20 metres in width, and its massive walls are preserved in some places to a height of four metres. The building is of a high standard, but it is not yet clear whether it formed part of the city's fortifications or whether it belonged to the palace complex which stood on the site—one more fascinating puzzle over which the archaeologists are pondering at the time of writing.

SECOND TEMPLE PERIOD: 37 B.C.E.–70 C.E.

Whoever finds himself today at the south-west corner of the Temple Mount, standing dwarfed by 13 metres of monumental Herodian blocks towering over him, readily takes Josephus' word for it when he described it as "a structure more noteworthy than any under the sun" (*Antiquities, XV, 413*). When one considers that this is merely the supporting wall with which Herod the Great built up the slopes and valleys surrounding the Temple Mount in order to enlarge the platform where the Temple itself was to stand, one's cement-and-steel-bound mind boggles at what the magnificence of the sanctuary must have been.

Three thousand years of history laid out at the southern wall of the Temple Mount.

Of the building upon and adjacent to the southern wall, Josephus left a most detailed description, the authenticity of which has now been confirmed by the excavations carried out in the area south and south-west of the Temple Mount. This testimony, added to the references to the Temple's southern approaches found in the Talmud, corroborate the archaeologists' finds, and provide a remarkably clear picture not only of the architectural form of the Temple Mount, but also of the everyday activities pursued around it during the reign of Herod. The digs carried out simultaneously in the Jewish Quarter—the Upper City of Second Temple times—have in their turn revealed a wealth of detail concerning the way of life of the city's well-to-do inhabitants during the same period.

From the time of King David, when as his capital Jerusalem first entered history as a national entity, the main entrance to the mount on which his son Solomon was to erect the First Temple was from the south. There may have been two reasons for this: the one practical, since the southern entrance was the nearest to the city itself, at that time situated on the slopes of the lower hill opposite; and the other psychological, the ascent towards the Holy of Holies having been counted on to impress the faithful. When Herod was set up by the Romans to rule over the Jews in 37 B.C.E., he sought to placate them for the loss of their already tenuous political independence of Hasmonean times by rebuilding the Temple on the same site and with the same orientation as those chosen by David and Solomon, and maintained by all their successors. Whatever his other qualities —or defects—Herod had a genius for building, a talent to which he gave free rein in his massive reconstruction of the Temple and its surroundings. By so doing he greatly enhanced the prestige of the site as the national, religious and economic centre of the vast Jewish diaspora which was scattered at the time throughout the Roman and Persian empires.

A contemporary of Christ making the pilgrimage to Jerusalem at Passover, Pentecost or on the Feast of Tabernacles was in fact well provided for. He could, if he wished, put up at one of the spacious hospices situated near the Temple's southern entrance, though if he was from abroad, he would probably seek lodgings in a centre maintained by his home community where his own language was spoken. Extensive remains of such centres have been found, the walls of their rooms finely plastered, the floors paved with neat mosaics and the stone ceilings domed in the typical local fashion.

Before entering the Temple Mount, the pilgrim was bound by religious injunction to purify his body—hence the large number of ritual baths (*mikva'ot*) installed, and still in evidence, all over the area. From the bathhouse, he would make his leisurely way across the

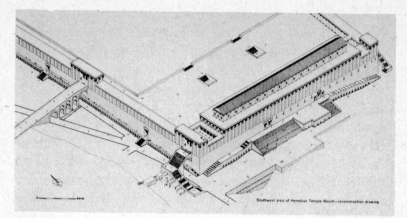

The south-western section of the Temple Mount as it might have looked in Herod's time. The reconstruction drawing shows the Royal Stoa running along the southern wall, the monumental staircase leading up to the Hulda Gates, the way up from the tunnels into the Temple Esplanade, and the elevated staircase leading into the Stoa from the west.

huge stone blocks which paved the public squares nearby, and mingle with the crowds who gathered there on the three pilgrim festivals. One can well imagine him gazing up, awestruck, at the Royal Stoa, a colonnaded portico running along the entire length of the southern wall and towering above him to a height of some 30 metres. While the Stoa itself was completely destroyed when the Romans burned the Temple, the fragments of capitals, lintels, friezes and panels which have survived attest to its magnificence.

Suitably humbled—perhaps he had listened to Christ addressing the wayward in the public square?—the pilgrim would ascend the monumental staircase, one of the most impressive finds of the recent excavations, up to the Hulda Gates. He could not hurry, for the 30, 65-metre-wide steps were alternately broad and narrow. Was not the Temple a holy place to be approached and departed from with dignity? He would enter the Esplanade by the eastern gate which was located on the same site as the present Triple Gate, and from there would pass through a tunnel which led beneath the Royal Stoa out onto the Esplanade itself. His devotions completed, he would leave by the tunnel leading to the western gate where the Double Gate now stands, just beneath the Al Aksa mosque.

Both of these tunnels exist today in an excellent state of preservation. In collaboration with the Waqf whose property they are, archaeologists have been able to study their cupolas and their ceiling decorations whose motives—geometrical and floral patterns with no faunal or human figures—are identical with those found on the fragments of the Royal Stoa. It is regrettable that these passages, an integral part of Herod's building conception, are closed to the general public. While only a *mezuza* (scroll fixed to doorposts of Jewish dwellings) on the lintel of the Triple Gate has survived from Herodian times, the original Double Gate is almost intact. Both gates were blocked by the Crusaders, presumably as a defensive measure, and so they have remained to this day.

On leaving the Temple Mount the pilgrim could stroll along the seven-metre-wide road which lay at the foot of the southern wall and led down a series of steps to the south-west corner of the Temple Mount, there to join its counterpart which ran along the western wall. If he had a sharp eye or a taste for beauty, he would observe the extraordinary dimensions of the paving stones—some as large as five metres by two—designed no doubt to maintain the proportions of the giant dressed ashlars with their elegantly finished margins of which the wall itself was built. In search of a gift to take home, he could meander down to the shops installed under the archways which served as a support for the steps above. If, on the other hand, he wished to catch a glimpse of the priests or the royal suite, the more to recount on his return home, he would continue to the south-west corner of the wall.

There a magnificent sight rose before him: a monumental stair-

Hebrew inscription on an ashlar found at the south-west corner of the Temple Mount: "To the place of trumpeting . . ."

case mounting from street level at the south and turning at right angles to enter the Royal Stoa from the west, passing high above the road at the foot of the western wall: in fact, a regal pedestrian flyover. Should it by chance have been the Sabbath eve, he could watch one of the high priests ascend the stairway to the tower that topped the Temple chambers at the south-west corner of the Mount, and from there sound the trumpet to indicate that the traditional day of rest had begun. The ashlar found lying on the street at the corner, exactly where it fell 2,000 years ago, is engraved with the words "To the place of trumpeting to . . . (declare?)" and was undoubtedly the cornerstone of the tower which Josephus described in detail in his prolific writings (*Wars,* IV, 582).

The discovery of the great staircase created a minor revolution in archaeological thinking. Until the recent digs, the arch which juts out from the western wall—named Robinson's Arch after the archaeologist who discovered it—was considered to be part of a viaduct across the Tyropeon Valley connecting the Temple Mount with the Upper City to the west. However, no trace of any such construction has ever been found. On the contrary, the tangible proofs of the stairway's existence—the series of descending piers on which it stood, the steps and the foundations—disprove the earlier theory. It now seems clear that the only causeway which led across the valley westwards was founded on Wilson's Arch which protrudes from the western wall further to the north.

Before leaving the city by the broad street leading north-westwards from the western wall, the pilgrim could do some more shopping at the boutiques grouped along the supporting arches of the great staircase, some of which have been partly reconstructed. His less fortunate 20th-century counterpart, if he cannot admire the original edifice in all its splendour, at least has the consolation of being able to study certain aspects of its construction, and follow up the subsequent history of the site.

Indeed, it is only as one observes at close quarters the 13 metres of perfectly preserved Herodian walls now revealed at the south-west corner that one can grasp how the structure resisted the attacks of the successive armies who fought over the city. The cornerstones, some weighing up to 70 tons, are made of a single block, one side of which is no less than eight metres long. This longer side is placed alternately on the western and southern sides, a smaller block dovetailing above to complete the corner. The strength of this construction was so great that no mortar was needed to join the stones, and no force ever succeeded in shifting them. The Romans quickly realised that only by setting it to the torch could they destroy the Temple, for the weakness of its monumental stones lay in the fact that they were made of limestone, and therefore inflammable. In fact, it is thanks to this method of destruction that the main road leading north-west along the western wall has been preserved. Only the thick layer of ash and chalk which covered the flagstones could have cushioned them against the shock of the gigantic burning blocks which toppled down onto them from the wall above, and lie today exactly as they fell.

The vast crowds of visitors who were attracted to Herod's renowned construction made the provision of an adequate water supply for drinking and ritual purification essential. This in turn involved the construction of a proportionate drainage system. Beneath the western wall, and more recently under the public squares at the southern wall, a series of wells, cisterns and massive aqueducts hewn into the bedrock have been revealed. As for the drainage system, it has been uncovered some seven metres below the Herodian street level at the south-west corner, complete with the conduits which led from the streets and squares above into the underground channels. South of the Double Gate are the exits of three overflow channels which were also part of the network. They run beneath the Al Aksa mosque and one of them was excavated in 1869 by Charles Warren. In 1968, the Waqf authorities blocked the channels, and they have not been touched since.

Large quantities of pottery, stoneware, lamps, cooking vessels, weights and coins, most of them minted in Jerusalem, came to light in the course of the excavations, many of them found in the cisterns and channels which fell into disuse after the destruction of the Temple. Some of the objects have the names of their owners engraved on them in Hebrew script. The most outstanding of the smaller finds, however, is the shard bearing the Hebrew word *korban*. The word means sacrifice and would seem to indicate that the vessel of which the vestige is a part was used in the Temple ritual. To some of the ornamental stone fragments grains of gold still obstinately adhere, further evidence of Josephus' precision when he spoke of the Sanctuary as being overlaid with stout plates of gold which blazed like fire in the early morning sun.

It was only natural that Jerusalem's well-to-do should seek to live as close as possible to the magnificent Temple Esplanade, and to enjoy the view out across it to the Mount of Olives and the hazy Judaean hills beyond. Until 1968, no one really believed that any Second Temple remains could possibly have survived the Roman ploughs which razed the Herodian city to the ground. However, partly as a result of the protective layer of ash which covered certain constructions, partly as a result of Herod's town planning, and partly inexplicably, the remains of three Herodian houses have survived

within 200 metres of the Temple Mount. That this area was part
of a wealthy residential suburb is indicated by the spaciousness of the
houses, their fine fresco and mosaic decorations, their complex
bathing installations and the high-quality building materials used
in their construction. The smaller articles—Phoenician glassware,
Roman amphorae, stone brought from abroad to be delicately
fashioned into household vessels—confirm the impression of ease
and elegance.

Unique in both size and splendour, the "Mansion" was undoubtedly
the home of a noble Jewish family. Occupying an area of over 600
square metres, the rooms were arranged around a central courtyard
as was customary at the time. The walls, of ashlar construction,
were at first decorated with colourful red and yellow frescoes depicting
architectural motifs, in this reminiscent of the style used at Pompeii.
Later, some were plastered over and, in what was probably the
reception room, redecorated with an incised pattern imitating

Shard bearing the Hebrew inscription *korban*, meaning sacrifice. It
was probably part of a vessel used in the Temple ritual.

Herodian masonry. Traces of the fire which raged through the house during the city's destruction lie in the charred wooden beams found on the floor of one of the rooms. Also on the ground floor of the Mansion a bathroom containing a small pool, at most a sitting bath, has been preserved, its mosaic floor depicting a six-petalled rosette in black and red having come down to us intact.

From the courtyard, in which the opening to a cistern was found, stairs led down to the basement level. Here were numerous stepped bathing pools vaulted in ashlar masonry, cisterns hewn into the bedrock, storerooms and a chequerboard mosaic at the entrance to one of the pools. These impressive installations indicate a high

The six-petalled mosaic rosette found on the floor of a bathroom in the "Mansion".

consumption of water in the house, the supply having probably been assured by the rainfall gathered on the Mansion's large expanses of roof and courtyard areas. Though not many small objects were discovered in this house, the few that remain attest to the status of its inhabitants. Notable among them are the fragments of a splendid glass jug, the finest produced at that period, made by the well-known Phoenician craftsman Ennion. Though found broken and distorted by the conflagration, the fragments are the more precious since only a very few of these vessels have survived to the present day.

The ground plan of what has been named the Herodian House, some 200 square metres in area, survived thanks to the demolition of its upper storeys to make way for the paving of a road, presumably one of the main thoroughfares which led from the Upper City to the road junction at the south-west corner of the Temple Mount. The street was simply laid directly over the ruins of the house. Here again the rooms lie round a central courtyard, with broad stairs leading down to a reservoir, partly vaulted over. Near the entrance to this stood a most interesting object: a stone with a bowl-like depression, in the centre of which is a knob surrounded by three perforations. This was probably a footbath of the type mentioned in the *Mishna* (*Yadaim*, 4:1), used for washing the feet before descending into the bathing pool. As with the Mansion, both the size of the structure and the elegant vessels found within it indicate a high standard of living. Besides the beautifully designed red sigillata ware were a large number of wine containers bearing Latin inscriptions—proof that the family liberally indulged its taste for imported Italian wine.

Remarkable in itself is the manner in which the basement of what has been named the "Burnt House" has been preserved. For some inexplicable reason it lay undisturbed throughout the centuries of building and rebuilding, to be uncovered in the 20th century exactly as it was left on the day of the fire in the year 70 C.E. Eloquent evidence of the tragedy are the skeletal remains of a young woman's right hand, outstretched as though imploring to be rescued from the kitchen in which the blaze had trapped her. Leaning against the wall ready for use in the battle was a spear. Its owner apparently did not have the time to grasp it before the flames overcame him.

Among the debris of scorched masonry, charred beams and thick ashes lay a large collection of pottery of all types, as well as many stone vessels—measuring cups, weights, pestles and mortars, and hand mills. These suggest that the building might have been used for some craft which involved measuring and grinding, unless of course this was simply part of the wealthy household. The common use of stone vessels, more expensive than pottery, as indicated in these and other finds, was no doubt due to the fact that in their ritual hygiene measures the Sages decreed them free of impurity.

It is considered more than likely that the "Burnt House," of which only a small area was accessible for excavation, belonged to the notorious Kathros family, for one of the stone weights found in it was incised with this name. The Talmud mentions the Kathros clan at length, for it was one of the large priestly families who abused their position by showing favouritism in granting duties within the Temple, and by generally exploiting the people. Thus, in *Pesahim*, 57: "Woe unto me from the House of Kathros . . . who are High Priests, and their sons are (Temple) treasurers, and their sons-in-law are (Temple) officers, and their slaves beat the people with rods." It is tempting, if not necessarily scientifically accurate, to imagine the wrath of the righteous aroused by the sight of the priestly Kathros's living it up in the most expensive part of town, their magnificent villa suspected of having been acquired out of public moneys. In any event, such a situation—not entirely unfamiliar to us today—fits in remarkably well with the picture of Jerusalem society as we know it in the time of Jesus and the Pharisees.

The public buildings which stood in the Upper City were apparently no less imposing than the private dwellings if one is to judge by the capitals and column bases strewn over the area. The most impressive among the capitals, carved in Ionic style, has a band of niche fluting around the attached column which is outstanding in its workmanship.

Of great significance in the history of glass-making techniques was the discovery of the refuse of a glass factory. This was preserved in the same manner as the Herodian house, and was found in a complex of reservoirs and baths covered by the paving stones of the same street. Among the fragments of moulded glass made in a process common at the time, were remains of blown glass, as well as tubes and bulbs which constitute the early stages of blown glass vessels. This is the first evidence ever found of the transitional period between the two methods of glass making, moulding and blowing, and, given the precision of the stratigraphical context fixed by the coins found together with the glass, it can now be confirmed that glass blowing began around the middle of the first century C.E.

Among the wealth and variety of smaller objects found in the Upper City are the earliest illustrations of the candelabrum which stood in the Temple. Incised as a decoration into the wall of a house, its tall branches, short stem and triangular base differ considerably from the *menora* depicted on the Arch of Titus in Rome as that brought back from the Temple in Jerusalem. Since this latter was carved some time after the Temple's destruction, it may be assumed that the fragment found bears a closer resemblance to the original candelabrum.

The finely decorated stone tables, small intricate bronze keys, elegantly turned stone vessels, and the skilfully painted frescoes and mosaics of which many fragments remain, all provide ample evidence of the degree of affluence reached by Jerusalem's upper class during the Second Temple period. It was not for nothing that Pliny the Elder described Jerusalem as "by far the most glorious city of the East and not of Judaea alone." Yet it was his countrymen who, by their thoroughgoing destruction of the rebellious Jewish

Design of a candelabrum found as a wall decoration. It is probably a more faithful reproduction of the *menora* which stood in the Temple than the one depicted on the Arch of Titus in Rome.

city, made sure that it would never again attain the degree of splendour which Herod bestowed upon it.

THE ROMAN PRESENCE—AELIA CAPITOLINA: 70–324 C.E.

Following the destruction of Jerusalem by Titus' legions and the subsequent depopulation of the city, nothing remained in the desolate area south of the Temple Mount but the huge supporting walls and the Double Gate with the stairs leading up to it. On the site which had formerly been the hub of Jewish life, the Tenth Legion was stationed as an occupation force; a large section of their camp has recently been uncovered. Many of the tiles and bricks bear the Tenth Legion's mark while others, dating from Hadrian's rebuilding of the city, were found stamped "Colonia Aelia Capitolina," Jerusalem's new Roman name. Of particular interest is the fragment of a pillar discovered in the foundations of the later Omayyad building nearby. It bears a Latin inscription on which the names of Vespasian and Titus clearly appear. Another inscription, engraved into a slab which originally paved the public square of Second Temple days, is dedicated to Septimus Severus.

A host of gems, seals and other objects were scattered over the area, among them bronze statues representing gods that were found in the rooms which served to worship them. One of these is identical with a figure discovered in a Roman camp on the Thames near London—eloquent testimony to the extent and presence of the Pax Romana. Among the 23,000 coins unearthed, some bear the *Judaea Capta* stamp. As for the large number of bone dice discovered, one would probably not be far wrong in assuming that the Roman Legionnaries found life in the deserted provincial outpost somewhat dull . . .

After the short-lived Jewish revolt against the Romans led by

Fragment of a Roman pillar bearing the names of Caesar Vespasian and Titus Caesar Vespasian.

Intaglio gems of the Roman period.

Bar Kochba (132–135 C.E.), the Emperor Hadrian determined to erase forever all trace of Jerusalem, hoping thus to destroy any possibility of Jewish irredentism. He ordered the remains of the city to be ploughed over, and built Aelia Capitolina on its ruins. As was the Roman custom, he laid out the former Upper City as if it were a military camp, with two main roads, the Cardo running north–south, and the Decummanus running east–west, dividing it into four quarters. That the Cardo roughly followed the line of what is still the Old City's main market, continuing along the main road into today's Jewish Quarter, was assumed from a most vivid depiction of the city found in a sixth-century mosaic in Madaba, Jordan. Laid in a church floor, the mosaic is part of a pictorial map of the Holy Land, and represents a bird's eye view of the city. The Cardo stands out as its centrepiece, appearing as a broad collonaded way running through the heart of the city between its northern and southern gates. Until about a year ago, no evidence had ever been found to confirm the precision of this map, and it was only in the course of the Jewish Quarter's reconstruction that it was "struck." What emerged was a well-paved road 13 metres wide, and clear evidence of a columned portico flanking it on either side. At the time of writing, further excavations are being carried out along the Cardo, and the passerby, watching fascinated as the earth is painstakingly brushed away, can speculate at will on just what will come to light this time . . . Needless to say, the plans for the reconstruction of the Street of the Jews were entirely modified in the light of the Cardo's remarkable discovery, and redrawn to incorporate it within the new building complex. A similar policy has been followed to preserve a 70-metre-long stretch of another Roman road found outside the Old City walls near the Dung Gate. The new road has been built above it, leaving the ancient route as a pedestrian underpass.

The Madaba mosaic map. In the centre of the upper section, Jerusalem is depicted as a walled city with the colonnaded Cardo running through it.

THE BYZANTINES: 324–638 C.E.

The conversion to Christianity of the Byzantine Emperor Constantine, who ruled over Jerusalem from 324 C.E., brought in its wake a new wave of building activity, consecrated this time to the embellishment of its Christian shrines. Constantine's mother, Queen Helena, a pagan likewise converted to Christianity, made a long stay in the city, by her presence undoubtedly raising its prestige and attracting to it a number of her son's well-born subjects.

The numerous remains of elegant terraced dwellings south of the Temple Mount, complete with baths, mosaic floors, arched doorways and rooms laid out around courtyards and gardens, attest to the existence of a fine residential quarter in the area which extended even beyond the present Ottoman city walls. A Greek mosaic, almost intact, can be seen in the floor of one of the houses near the Herodian stairway to the Double Gate, its inscription invoking a blessing on the house's inhabitants. Many of the bricks and tiles used in these constructions bear the trademark of Greek artisans. One particularly large construction further eastwards is thought to have been a hospice for pilgrims, while nearby a section of the defensive wall of the quarter has also survived. Along the courses of the Herodian western wall one can distinguish traces of the piping through which water was brought to the Byzantine bathhouse found opposite Robinson's arch, but at a higher stratigraphical level than the Herodian remains.

It was in this period too that the Hebrew inscription from *Isaiah* 66:14, mentioned earlier, was engraved into the western wall below Robinson's arch. This may indeed be a reflection of the revival of Jewish national feeling during the reign of Julian in the fourth century when he made plans for the rebuilding of the Temple, a project which died with him. The Jewish decorations found on the walls of some of the Byzantine houses have lead the archaeologists to believe that Jews resettled in the former Christian houses in the seventh century following the Persian conquest.

The Madaba map again proved valuable in the identification of a set of massive foundations found in the Jewish Quarter. The presence of existing buildings has prevented their complete excavation, but the apse, the massive masonry and the situation of the ruins as compared with the mosaic, indicate that these are the remains of the famous Nea Cathedral built by Justinian in 543 C.E., and destroyed by an earthquake in the eighth century. Both the descriptions of contemporary pilgrims and historian Procopius' accounts confirm this assumption. Just outside the Ottoman walls, a corner of the Cathedral has been revealed, while the series of rooms adjacent to it would appear to be the hospital and pilgrims' hospice mentioned in historical documents. This discovery has put an end to centuries of speculation as to where the Nea Basilica actually stood, and constitutes a find rich in significance for the early history of the Christian church.

THE EARLY MOSLEM PERIOD: 638–1099 C.E.

Even more dramatic was the uncovering, above the Byzantine ruins south of the Temple Mount, of a vast building complex belonging to the Omayyad period (660–750 C.E.). Unlike the Second Temple or Byzantine finds, there was absolutely no written evidence to indicate that these buildings had ever existed, so that their discovery came as a complete surprise both to Israel's archaeologists and to the Moslem world. In all, six enormous structures have been revealed. They were clearly an integral part of the extensive religious centre set up in Jerusalem by the Omayyad Caliphs, of which the Dome of the Rock and the Al Aksa mosques on the Temple Mount were the central pivots.

An aerial view of the Omayyad remains . . .

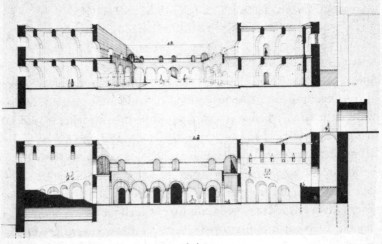

. . . and a reconstruction drawing of them.

The most outstanding of the six is considered to have been the palace used by the Caliphs when they visited Jerusalem, for from its roof an overhead footway spanned the street below to lead directly into the Al Aksa mosque. All the buildings lay around central court-yards bordered by cloisters from which a series of rooms led off, a form of architecture common in the region at the time. The structures surrounding the palace might have been used as khans for high ranking visitors, houses of study, bathhouses or storerooms. The sophisticated system of water collection and drainage discovered is as impressive as the rest of the complex.

The decorations of the Omayyad buildings as revealed in the sur-viving fragments bear only floral and geometrical patterns, the faunal and human motives in evidence elsewhere being completely absent. Neither did the construction contain any towers, for it was placed within the outer city walls and did not require any further defenses. Among the stones used were many from the Second Temple which the Moslem builders re-employed. Significant is the fact that, hard by the Hebrew inscription from *Isaiah* mentioned above, is a seventh century Arabic one praising Allah the Merciful.

The entire Omayyad complex disappeared, like the Nea Cathedral, in the disastrous eighth-century earthquake, and the rise of the Abbasids thereafter put paid to Omayyad aspirations for Jerusalem. The ruins, rich in building materials, first became a quarry, but by the 11th century the site had been turned into a cemetery. From then on it fell into a wretched state, the very memory of the splendid Moslem edifice buried in oblivion for 1,000 years until its recent rediscovery.

THE CRUSADERS: 1099–1187 C.E.

Jerusalem shrank considerably during Crusader times, comprising an area no larger than that covered today by the Old City. Thus the

The Church of St. Mary of the Teutonic Knights in the heart of the Jewish Quarter has been restored, and laid out as an archaeological garden.

southern section, scene of such splendour in Herodian and Omayyad times, was outside its boundaries, the southern wall of the Temple Mount being used for the first time as the city's outer defensive wall. Thus it was that the Double and Triple Gates were blocked, and a defensive tower built adjacent to the walls of the Al Aksa mosque, the remains of which are still clearly in evidence.

Outside the Dung Gate, a most impressive network of Crusader fortifications, out of which the Ottoman walls were to sprout in their turn, have been brought to light. Among the series of towers, one has been identified as the Tanneries Tower which figures in ancient maps. It was so named because it served as a postern gate for the tanners whose workshops adjoined the Crusader cattle market, located on what are today the approaches to the Western Wall. Further west, just inside the Ottoman walls in the Jewish Quarter, another large-scale Crusader edifice is in the course of excavation, though just exactly what it is has yet to be determined.

In the very heart of the Jewish Quarter itself are to be found the delightful vestiges of the Crusader church known as St. Mary of the Teutonic Knights. Mentioned in mediaeval documents, the centre was known to have contained, besides the church itself, a hospital and a hospice. The remains of the halls that housed them are still clearly distinguishable on the different floors of the structure. The church, located just above the steps leading down to the Western Wall, is of typical romanesque style, its three halls ending in semi-circular apses whose windows commanded a magnificent view of the Mount of Olives. The site has been completely restored in order to reflect faithfully this period of Jerusalem's history, and an archaeological garden has been laid out within it for the benefit of pilgrims, tourists, and Jerusalemites alike.

* * *

With the Ottoman conquest and the rebuilding of the mighty city walls by Suleiman the Magnificent in the mid-16th century, Jerusalem's past emerges above ground. Preserved almost intact, the ramparts, whose crenellations, gates and towers are so finely adapted to the hilly contours of the land, have now recovered their former splendour. Pinkish gold in the sunshine, ethereal in moonlight, they stand superb and, like a theatrical backdrop, unmoved by the four centuries of human drama that have been enacted at their feet.

As the treasures hidden in Jerusalem's storehouse of antiquity come to light one by one, the world's knowledge of ancient Jerusalem, and the cultural heritage of Jews, Christians and Moslems throughout the ages continues to advance. Indeed, more has been made known in the past ten years of research than in the preceding century of small-scale archaeological digs. Better than all the learned volumes, the remains dug up out of the earth demonstrate the constant inter-penetration of the three great religions within the city of Jerusalem. Perhaps, in the course of time, they will help to contribute to a better understanding of each by the other, putting an end once and for all to the bloody strife which has torn at the city for so long. It is too much to hope that 2,000 years from now, archaeologists will find no further remains preserved under the ashes of their own destruction?

CHANGING
LIVING
PATTERNS

RELIGIOUS LIFE

"NOT A synagogue, but a place more interesting than any synagogue in the world, is a small court near the south-west corner of the wall inclosing the area of the mosque of Omar. This is the Jews' Wailing Place. Here, on any Friday evening, may be witnessed a sight unparalleled for peculiarity and pathos. Against the massive stones of the old wall, that were probably built by the master masons of Herod, men and women stand and read their prayers and weep as their forefathers wept at Babylon. On a day when the weather permits, as many as two hundred will assemble in this small court to beseech Heaven to 'have mercy on Zion.' This place, just outside, is as near as any Jew will approach to the Temple area. They fear to enter the inclosure lest they tread on the place where once stood the 'Holy of Holies.' This practice of gathering at the Wailing Place began in the Middle Ages. During all these years the same litany has been chanted and the same prayers read. And the end is not yet. No one who has carefully watched this service at the wall can doubt the religious sincerity of the majority who participate in it. They are as genuinely earnest and as truly devout as people can be. Whatever one may think of the practice, or whatever his feeling towards the

Pious Jews and mitred monks pursue their devotions unhindered.

race whose members indulge in it, their earnestness in prayer and devotion to a seemingly hopeless task cannot fail to awaken in him a feeling of sympathy. Hopeless it is, and the closing years of the nineteenth century furnish no prophecy that it will ever be otherwise.

"In this City of the Jews, where the Jewish population outnumbers all others three to one, the Jew has few rights that the Mohammedan or average Christian is bound to respect. For example, he dare not pass along the street on which the so-called Church of the Holy Sepulcher fronts. A Jew unacquainted with this restriction was making his way along this thoroughfare recently. Being observed by some Greek Christians, he was set upon and would undoubtedly have been killed but for the timely intervention of some Turkish police. However, the police did not arrest his assailants, nor was any effort made to punish them."

Thus wrote Edwin S. Wallace, former United States Consul in Jerusalem, in an article published in the monthly *Cosmopolitan* in 1899. Were Mr. Wallace to return to the scene he so vividly described, not on a Friday evening, but at the solemnest moment in in the Jewish religion's liturgy, sunset on Yom Kippur, he would probably not believe he was in the same place. The "small court" he refers to is now a vast open square, and at the last moment before God is believed to seal the destiny of each and every Jew for the coming year, thousands flock freely to it from all directions in a final act of repentance. The earnestness and sincerity he observed are as powerful as before, but they are heightened today by a renewed sense of dignity born of the spirit of freedom in which worship at the Wall is conducted. What would surely surprise Mr. Wallace the most, however, is that, as the fatal hour approaches, the tinkling of church bells sounding Vespers can be heard above the continuo of Jewish chants. A short while later, only seconds before the conclusion of the day when the dramatic sound of the shofar rings out across the square, the muezzin from atop the minaret hard by the Western Wall in turn calls Mohammed's faithful to prayer.

In the light of the centuries of religious persecution to which the Jews have been subjected, it was only natural that, on finding themselves in possession of the sites holy to Christianity and Islam, they would guarantee complete freedom of worship to members of both these sister faiths. In 1967, the Protection of the Holy Places law was enacted guaranteeing the sites themselves against violation, and ensuring freedom of access to them by members of the various religions. Furthermore, each religious authority was granted full internal autonomy.

That the 1967 law has been scrupulously applied can be seen at all hours of the day or night by anyone walking through the streets of the Old City. On a Friday, busloads of festively dressed Moslems from Hebron make their way up to the Temple Mount, while at the Western Wall beneath, pious Jews spiritually prepare themselves to welcome the Shabbat. Monks and nuns pass quietly by, on their way to the Via Dolorosa. More significant still, in the past decade hundreds of thousands of Moslems from all parts of the Arab world have been allowed freely to enter Israel and pray at their shrines, irrespective of the political attitudes taken by their respective governments in the Israel–Arab dispute.

The religious communities in Jerusalem are completely autonomous and enjoy equal status. As in Ottoman and British Mandatory times, matters of personal status—marriage, divorce, inheritance—come under the jurisdiction of the religious courts of each community which, in their turn, enjoy full autonomy and equal status. The Sabbaths and festivals of Christianity and Islam, along with the Jewish Shabbat, are recognised as official holidays for members of the respective faiths so that, in fact, Jerusalem's shops are all open at the same time only four days a week: the Moslems close on Friday, the Jews on Saturday and the Christians on Sunday.

The *status quo,* drawn up in Ottoman times, is based on the assumption that the responsibility for the administration of the Christian holy places devolves upon the churches themselves, and it defines the rights and possessions of each one of them within the holy places. This ruling remained in force throughout the Mandatory period and has been maintained since 1967. In exceptional cases, where friction has arisen among the 17 Christian institutions represented in Jerusalem, Israel authorities have helped them reach a compromise.

The administration of all Moslem property and affairs is the responsibility of the Supreme Moslem Council. Since 1969, security on the Temple Mount has been assured by Jerusalem Moslem members of the Israel police force under the orders of a Moslem officer. The Supreme Moslem Council enjoys formal status and its authority is officially recognised. Its executive arm, the Waqf, functions without any interference whatsoever by any Israel body.

Immediately after the Six Day War, Israel undertook the restoration and repair of Church property damaged during the 1948 and 1967 hostilities, regardless of the exact cause of the damage. Since then, relations between Israel authorities and the religious bodies have been cordial and businesslike. The Ministry of Religious Affairs takes care of the practical needs of the churches vis-à-vis the Israel administration, and the Jewish National Fund's Afforestation Department distributes annually 20,000 Christmas trees as a gift to the Christian population.

At the municipal level, Church property has by mutual agreement been made available to enhance the beauty of the city, while on the

The Armenian Theological Seminary recently constructed in the Old City.

The Lutheran Centre on the Mount of Olives and . . .

. . . the Ecumenical Institute in south Jerusalem, both built since 1967.

other hand the city has facilitated the development of Christian activity within it. Since 1967, a number of important religious institutions have sprouted on the Jerusalem scene. Just south of the city lies the Vatican's Ecumenical Institute where Christian theologians from all parts of the world meet and share their experiences with the intention of achieving their eventual reunion. In the Armenian Quarter of the Old City an impressive Theological Seminary has been built, while in Beit Hanina a Roman Catholic church and community centre has been set up. The Lutheran Federation also plans to build a study centre on the Mount of Olives. As for the Greek Orthodox Church, it has restored its ancient monastery in the Valley of the Cross and has turned it into a seminary. Two new mosques have been erected in Jerusalem since 1967, bringing their total number to 36. Influenced no doubt by the feverish activity in the city at large, the Church and Waqf authorities have in their turn undertaken the restoration of their respective monuments, among them the Al Aksa mosque and the mediaeval cotton market in the Moslem Quarter which are being renovated by the Supreme Moslem Council.

It is worthy of note that between 1948 and 1967 the Christian population of Jordanian-ruled Jerusalem dwindled rapidly, partly as a result of the systematic bans and restrictions imposed upon it on religious grounds. From a population 25,000 in 1948, it fell to 10,795 in 1967. Since then, this tendency has been reversed, the Christian population having increased steadily over the ten years of Israel administration to reach 12,000 in 1976. The Moslem population has maintained its previous rate of increase, growing from 60,000 in 1967 to 84,000 in 1976.

The new spirit of religious tolerance which has reigned in Jerusalem since 1967 has led, among other things, to a certain rapprochement between Judaism and Christianity, making the city a kind of laboratory of unity. The Hebrew-speaking Dominican brothers plan to establish a centre for Jewish studies in which Christians will be able to study

Jewish reality at all levels—Biblical, religious and national. They consider it a great advantage to be able to benefit from the Jews' subjective approach to the Bible, and the sense of urgency which the Scriptures take on in the realistic world in which they are read. The Rainbow Group, composed of Jewish and Christian scholars, meets regularly, while the Interfaith committee has been set up as Israel's representative to the many groups of Christians who visit Israel annually. It is significant that the first international meeting of the steering committee of the World Council of Churches and the Jewish Committee, the two joined later by the Vatican Committee, was held in Jerusalem ten years after reunification. One can only regret that political influences have so far prevented a similar process from getting under way between Moslem and Jewish theologians.

The mediaeval cottom market in the Moslem Quarter since its restoration by the Waqf authorities.

ECONOMIC EXPANSION AND INTEGRATION

The opening up of Jerusalem to free economic activity after its reunification brought increased prosperity to all concerned. The sleepy tourist business, principal source of revenue in east Jerusalem and a minor item in the western sector before 1967, has become a booming enterprise throughout the city, while for both Jewish and Arab businessmen, Jerusalem has resumed its natural role as the link between Israel and the broad markets of Judaea and Samaria. Goods and services move freely in both directions, with Israel firms represented in Arab-populated areas, Arab exports transitting through Jerusalem to Israel's ports, and Arab services widely employed in the Jewish commercial and administrative sectors.

A direct result of economic integration was the great increase in salaries earned by Arab workers employed by Israel enterprises, this in accordance with the law enforcing equal pay for equal work. Despite the steep rise in prices in east Jerusalem which followed reunification, it is estimated that the average Arab wage-earner has increased his real income by some 150 per cent. Following Israel norms, Arab employers in their turn raised their workers' salaries. This process, added to the implementation of the principles of a modern welfare state from which all Israel's citizens benefit, has contributed to a more even distribution of income among the Arab population, the poor getting richer and the rich—a little less rich. Another outstanding evolution in the socio-economic pattern of Jerusalem's Arabs' life since 1967 has been the employment of women in the labour force. Their contribution to the household budget has not only improved their families' living standards, but has also meant a change in the traditional status of women in the city's Arab society.

Of the Arab population's total labour force of 18,000, about one-third are employed in east Jerusalem. Eight thousand are members of the Histadrut, Israel's Labour Federation, and enjoy protection and benefits identical with those of their Jewish counterparts.

One of the most serious obstacles encountered on the way to

Jews and Arabs on the job during the building boom.

economic integration was the tax issue. The city's Jordanian citizens had been accustomed to paying low taxes, in return for which they received a low level of services and no social security at all. Israel's system is the reverse and has had to be introduced gradually in order to ease the transition. After a tough initial period, most commercial enterprises in east Jerusalem are now making good profits, often higher than those they registered before 1967. Certain luxury boutiques, however, have had stiff competition to face from Israeli competitors. In 1967, a IL 15,000,000 revolving fund was set up from which two-year loans are granted to Arab businessmen for commercial and industrial expansion.

Industrial expansion in Jerusalem was given a great boost after 1967, eight times more industrial space having since been required annually than in the years prior to reunification. To meet this demand, two industrial zones were constructed on former border areas, one at Talpioth and the other, a science-based industry complex, near Sanhedria. A third zone is located at Atarot on the city's present northern border. The Talpioth and Atarot zones are available for the implantation of both Jewish and Arab industries providing they are non-polluting, and serve as a source of employment for hundreds of Arab workers. However, the basic employment distribution of Jerusalem's population will continue to be characteristic of a capital city and tourist centre, with only some 17 per cent of its labour force employed in industry, 50 percent in government institutions and universities, and the remaining 33 per cent in tourism and services.

THE ADMINISTRATION OF EAST JERUSALEM

Since 1967 the Israel Government and the Jerusalem Municipality have aimed to establish a uniform network of services throughout the city. In many respects this objective has already been achieved or is well on the way to realisation, as the survey on pages 26–28 above shows. In the social and cultural spheres, the city fathers and those associated with them have opted, after a long period of soul-searching, for a policy of gradual transition from one way of life to another. This approach finds expression in a series of practical arrangements such as the gradual imposition of the Israel fiscal system, the possibility for the city's Arab citizens to maintain ties with the Jordanian Government, the introduction of a tailor-made secondary education programme to fit local needs, and the creation almost out of nothing of cultural facilities for the Arab-speaking population.

Less easy to define is an overall attitude which endeavours to respect traditional family patterns and social values, and to protect them from too rapid an erosion by the criteria of the modern "consumer" society. In this, as in the other fields mentioned, it is felt that a natural course of evolution is preferable to the immediate imposition of measures or ways of life which will be neither understood nor accepted by a population whose background and traditions differ in so many ways from those of the men responsible for the quality of life in their city.

The Arab sector of Jerusalem is administered by the Municipality's Department for East Jerusalem Affairs. This division has absorbed into its ranks some thousand employees, half of them of the former Jordanian Municipality, and although its role is limited to city matters, it in fact serves as a liaison office between the capital's Arab citizens and Israel's national administration.

Contact is maintained between the city authorities and the Arab neighbourhoods—13 municipal quarters and 14 villages—through the mukhtar, frequently their traditional head. However, an effort is being made to develop young, democratically elected leadership in the villages. At all times, the mukhtar is actively encouraged to fulfill his role in the promotion of the interests of the neighbourhood and the population he represents. Every Friday Jerusalem's Arabs flock to the Department for East Jerusalem Affairs to submit their requests and complaints, this in a spirit of complete freedom and equality. Like their Jewish co-citizens, they voted in large numbers during the last municipal elections.

The East Jerusalem Chamber of Commerce acts as a liaison office between the Arab population and the Jordanian Government for all technical, economic and personal matters which are the consequence of 19 years of Jordanian administration over the city. Since Jerusalem's Arab citizens, though automatically residents of the city, have been given the choice between Israel and Jordanian citizenship, the Chamber of Commerce fulfills an essential role in the lives of those who have opted for the latter. Four daily newspapers appear in Jerusalem in Arabic, one enjoying Government support, the other three put out privately and independently by Arab publishers.

EDUCATION

The most urgent task which confronted the Jerusalem Municipality in 1967 was to provide adequate facilities for the application of Israel's education system in the eastern sector of the city. Education authorities were faced with a dire lack of classrooms and a total absence of pre-school education. Within ten years, the total number of classrooms has almost doubled (from 230 to 440), some 50 kindergartens have been created, ten elementary schools built or renovated, and three vocational schools established. Further, a master plan has been drawn up to ensure that future needs will be adequately catered for.

The introduction of pre-school education between the ages of five and six was a new idea for the Arab population to assimilate. Today, however, its advantages are recognised and the principle widely accepted. If the number of children who frequent them—1,600 —appears to be a fairly small proportion of the total Arab school population, it should be recalled that by tradition, since Ottoman through Mandatory days, some 40 per cent of Jerusalem's Arab children have been educated at independent private or Church schools. This situation has not changed since 1967.

In the elementary and junior high schools run by the city, nearly 12,000 Arab children follow the same curriculum as that of Israel's Arab population. Studies are conducted in Arabic and are based on Arab educational elements such as the Koran, the history and geography of the Arab world, Arab literature and so on.

For the secondary schools a different solution was found. For many years Jerusalem's Arab families have sent their children abroad to Arab universities to study. However, these institutions do not accept the matriculation certificate granted by Israel education authorities, despite the fact that Israel recognises those issued by Arab secondary schools. Since Israel wished to maintain the existing tradition, and at the same time to give Jerusalem's Arab youth the choice between Israel and Arab institutions of higher learning, it has evolved a programme of study which meets the requirements of both. It is based on the regular Arab high school curriculum, with the addition of Hebrew language and Israel civics, courses designed to ease integration into Israel society. The only alteration Israel has made in the Arab programme is the expurgation from textbooks of their former virulent, anti-Israel contents. With the matriculation certificate obtained at the end of this study programme, the Arab student is thus free to choose between an Israel or Arab university. For those who opt directly for Israel institutions of higher learning, a special school offers the standard Israel secondary school curriculum. Since the implementation of this dual education system in 1976, the number of Arab students attending municipal high schools has increased by 40 per cent, from 694 to 1,050, this following a considerable drop in their numbers between 1967 and 1975. These figures clearly indicate that the course followed corresponds to the desires of the population. Again by tradition, secondary education has remained free for Arab pupils, prejudicing them most favourably vis-à-vis their Jewish counterparts.

A growing number of Arab youths are attending the vocational training schools newly established for them, this type of education greatly facilitating their integration within the labour force. This year, the Municipality intends to assist the private schools financially in the provision of similar courses, as well as Hebrew language programmes.

HEALTH AND WELFARE

Jerusalem's Arabs benefit from exactly the same health services as the Jewish population and under the same conditions, namely, membership of one of the national sick funds. The largest of these, the Kupat Holim which is run by the Histadrut, has established a clinic for its 6,000 members in east Jerusalem, though its centres in the north and north-eastern suburbs are of course available to them. Non-members in dire straits can apply for medical assistance to the city's Social Welfare Department.

Municipal public health and dental services cover all schools throughout the city. Since 1967, when all Arab schoolchildren were given a thorough check-up, the necessary vaccinations administered and the existing trachoma and malnutrition cases dealt with, their health has reached the same level as that of Jewish youngsters. Three mother-and-child centres have been set up in Arab neighbourhoods. Completely new to them, the Arab mothers have taken quickly to the system and the centres are now highly frequented. The East Talpioth and Givat Shapira centres serve both Jewish and Arab mothers, creating a natural meeting point between them.

It is in the realm of social welfare that the greatest improvement in life among the Arab population has been felt. In 1967, some 70

needy families received sporadic assistance from the Jordanian authorities. Today, no fewer than 6,000 families receive regular monthly
payments from Israel's National Insurance Fund, representing some
IL 14,000,000 annually. This sum includes outright welfare payments
as well as old-age pensions, despite the fact that the beneficiaries of
the latter paid into the fund for only five years of their active life.
Participation in the National Insurance Fund has been introduced
gradually, and the Arab population is becoming accustomed to con-
tributing to it. Municipal welfare payments to a further 800 families
total IL 4,000,000 annually.

CULTURAL AND SOCIAL ACTIVITIES

The Municipality of Jerusalem, in conjunction with the Jerusalem
Foundation, has shown considerable imagination in its efforts to
equate the cultural facilities of its Jewish and Arab citizens. Among
the kind of problems they have had to solve was how to enable all
Arab schoolchildren to attend one concert and one theatrical per-
formance a year, as stipulated by the city's cultural programme, when
neither an Arab orchestra nor an Arab theatre existed in the city.
Today an Arab municipal theatre is in the process of formation with,
as its core, an existing troupe of semi-professional actors. As for
musical education, research is being carried out into the origins of
Arab folk music in order to create a repertoire which could be
accepted as a basis for Arab children's musical education.

In the artistic field, a youth programme parallel to that offered by
the Israel Museum is to be organised at the Rockefeller Museum near
the Arab suburbs. The programme will be offered in Arabic, as well
as in Hebrew for the children living in the northern and north-
eastern suburbs. The plastic art activities, where language is no
barrier, will provide a meeting ground for both groups. All Arab

children make their annual obligatory visits to art and cultural exhibitions at either the Israel or the Rockefeller Museums. Eventually it is hoped to create a Jerusalem Centre for Arabic Arts which will house the newly formed orchestra and theatre, and will serve as a cultural foyer for Jerusalem's Arabs in the same way as the Jerusalem Theatre caters to Jewish cultural needs.

Of the 12 new libraries built in Jerusalem since 1967, three of them are devoted to Arab literature and are located in Arab-speaking

Beit David, community centre for Arab youth. Under Jewish administration, it has a record 2,000 members, and a daily attendance of 400.

neighbourhoods. One of them, in the ancient village of Silwan, previously served as a goat pen. Cleaned and whitewashed with the help of the villagers themselves, its vaulted roof now shelters a well-stocked library which is highly frequented by children and grown-ups alike. One of the city's three mobile libraries serves outlying Arab villages. Another improvement in the quality of life in Jerusalem's Arab suburbs are the ten parks and playgrounds that have been newly laid out, a luxury unknown in Jordanian days.

In conjunction with the Municipality and the Jerusalem Foundation, the International Cultural Centre for Youth (ICCY) runs two community centres for Arab youth jointly with its original one in west Jerusalem. Under recognised Jewish administration, the Centre's staff is made up of young Arabs trained by the ICCY. The success of these centres has surpassed the most optimistic previsions, the first of the two, Beit David, with 2,000 members and enjoying a daily attendance of some 400, youths and adults alike. The centres' activities are many and varied, and regular exchanges take place between them and the mother centre. All this helps to widen the horizons of their members, as much with regard to Israel realities as to the world at large.

To help encourage Jerusalem's youth to get together, events such as the Youth Festival, the Youth City and an art exhibition are organised annually for members of all the municipal community centres. At these gatherings, the various groups put on theatrical and variety shows—simultaneous translation is provided—and display their handiwork. Sporting events, in which teams from all over the city participate, also constitute a favourable meeting ground for the city's citizens of tomorrow.

COMMON
DESTINY

THAT JERUSALEM in 1977, a decade after its return to Jewish sovereignty, is well on the way to being reunited in the urbanistic, economic and municipal spheres, there can be little doubt. With meticulous care, its cultural heritage has been unearthed and preserved, irrespective of its origin, while religious life has been pursued by all within its walls in complete freedom and security.

The only domain which cannot be measured, or submitted to the planner's slide-rule, is that which lies in the hearts of men. It could hardly be expected that in such a short time the deepseated antagonisms born of the long, bitter conflict between Israel and her Arab neighbours would be completely eradicated. On the other hand, there were many Cassandras who predicted the direst consequences following the reunification of Jerusalem's Jewish and Arab sectors in 1967. These prophecies have not materialised. Apart from isolated acts of violence committed by subversive elements from outside the city in an attempt to disrupt life within it, Jerusalem has been calm in the past decade. More significantly, it was in no way disrupted during the Yom Kippur War in 1973 when passions were running high elsewhere in the Middle East.

Today, contact between the two populations is carried out in a businesslike manner, sometimes to the satisfaction of both parties,

In a city reborn . . .

. . . to live and let live.

sometimes not. But is that not in the nature of any form of human relations? Whatever the political opinions held by the Arab population of Jerusalem, it seems clear to those who know them well that they are fully aware of the improvements that have taken place in their living conditions in the past ten years, and of the advantages that have accrued to them from living in a reunited, free and open city. As time has gone by, they have modified their image of Israel from a many-headed monster to a reality with which one can deal. Both sides have sought avenues of practical cooperation on a day-to-day basis in accordance with their mutual interests, and the picture the city presents today is adequate proof that in most cases they have succeeded.

Ideally situated on the watershed between two worlds, Jerusalem should, in the next ten years, become a microcosmic model of how many ethnic groups, some of them former enemies, can, through a policy of enlightened self-interest and reciprocal goodwill, find ways to peacefully pursue their common destiny in the city, living and letting live.

MAIN EVENTS IN THE HISTORY OF JERUSALEM

B.C.E.

1,000–961 David establishes Jerusalem as the capital of the united Kingdom of Israel

961–922 King Solomon reigns and builds the First Temple on the site chosen by his father David

587 Jerusalem and the First Temple are destroyed by Nebuchadnezzar and the Jews exiled to Babylon

537 Return of the Jews from Babylon

515 Reconstruction of the Temple

320 Ptolomey I enters Jerusalem

198 Seleucids occupy the city and plunder the Temple

167 Jewish Revolt led by the Hasmoneans following the desecration of the Temple by Antiochus Epiphanes

164 Judas Maccabeus liberates Jerusalem and rededicates the Temple

63 Pompey of Rome captures Jerusalem

37 Herod the Great appointed King to succeed Antigonus, the last Hasmonean who ruled briefly between 40 and 37. Herod rebuilds Jerusalem and the Temple

4 Death of Herod

C.E.

6	Jerusalem becomes part of the province of Judaea and is governed by a Roman procurator
33	Crucifixion of Jesus
66–70	War of the Jews against Rome ends in the fall of Jerusalem and the destruction of the Temple by Titus
132–135	Second Jewish Revolt led by Bar Kochba
135	Roman Emperor Hadrian razes Jerusalem to the ground and builds Aelia Capitolina on its site. Jews are forbidden to enter the city
326	Queen Helena, mother of Byzantine Emperor Constantine, visits Jerusalem and a period of extensive building of Christian holy sites begins
614	Persians conquer Jerusalem
629	Byzantine rule is re-established
638	Caliph Omar captures Jerusalem
691	The Dome of the Rock is completed
750	Omayyads succeeded by Abbasids of Baghdad
969	Fatimid caliphs of Egypt succeed Abbasids
1009	Caliph Hakim orders the destruction of Christian churches
1077	Seljuk Turks take over Jerusalem from the Egyptians
1099	The First Crusade. Jerusalem is captured by Godfrey de Bouillon and the Latin Kingdom established
1187	Saladin captures Jerusalem from the Crusaders
1244	Jerusalem is sacked by the Tartars
1347	Jerusalem is reconquered by the Mamelukes
1517	Ottoman conquest of Jerusalem by Selim I
1538–1540	Suleiman the Magnificent rebuilds the city ramparts
1838	The first British Consulate is opened in Jerusalem
1859	The first Jewish settlement is established outside the Old City walls

1917 The British conquest of Jerusalem by General Allenby is followed by British Mandatory rule in 1922

1925 The Hebrew University is inaugurated on Mt. Scopus

1948 The British Mandate is terminated, the State of Israel is proclaimed and is followed by Israel's War of Independence

1949 The Israel–Transjordan Armistice agreement divides Jerusalem between the two countries; new Jerusalem is declared capital of the State of Israel

June 7, 1967 Israel troops enter the Old City and Jerusalem is reunited

SELECTED BIBLIOGRAPHY

Jerusalem, Sacred City of Mankind: Teddy Kollek and Moshe Pearlman, Steimatsky, Jerusalem, 1968.

Jerusalem: Keter Publishers, Jerusalem 1973.

Developing Jerusalem 1967–1975: David Krojanker, Jerusalem Foundation, 1975.

The Jochanan ben Zakkai Synagogues: Jerusalem Foundation.

Jerusalem Revealed: The Israel Exploration Society, Jerusalem, 1975.

Archeological Discoveries in the Jewish Quarter of Jerusalem: N. Avigad, the Israel Exploration Society and the Israel Museum, 1976.

Jerusalem, Holy City of Three Religions: R. J. Zwi Werblowsky, Yuval Press, Jerusalem, 1976.

Jerusalem, a Geopolitical Imperative: Saul B. Cohen, article in *Midstream*, May 1976.

Jerusalem Post articles by Abraham Rabinowich.

The Jerusalem Committee Report, 1975.